THE COMPLETE FINANCIAL LITERACY COLLECTION: 2 BOOKS IN 1

A FUN & EASY STEP-BY-STEP GUIDE FOR KIDS, TEENS & YOUNG ADULTS TO MASTER SMART MONEY HABITS, ACHIEVE FINANCIAL SECURITY AND GROW WEALTH WITH EASE

MONEY MENTOR PUBLICATIONS

TABLE OF CONTENTS

THE ULTIMATE GUIDE TO FINANCIAL LITERACY FOR KIDS
MASTER MONEY SKILLS WITH FUN AND INTERACTIVE WAYS TO SAVE, BUDGET, SPEND WISELY, AND INVEST WITH CONFIDENCE
MONEY MENTOR PUBLICATIONS

A STRESS-FREE GUIDE TO FINANCIAL LITERACY FOR TEENS & YOUNG ADULTS

MASTER MONEY MANAGEMENT, AVOID COSTLY MISTAKES, INVEST LIKE A PRO, AND SECURE YOUR FINANCIAL FUTURE

MONEY MENTOR PUBLICATIONS

THE ULTIMATE GUIDE TO FINANCIAL LITERACY FOR KIDS

MASTER MONEY SKILLS WITH FUN AND INTERACTIVE WAYS TO SAVE, BUDGET, SPEND WISELY, AND INVEST WITH CONFIDENCE

MONEY MENTOR PUBLICATIONS

INTRODUCTION

All right, friends, gather around! Let me tell you a story about Alex. Alex had been saving up allowances and birthday money for what felt like forever, eyeing this super cool, almost magical remote-controlled drone. But then, out of the blue, a shiny new video game caught Alex's eye, threatening to derail all those months of saving. The struggle was real: to save or to spend, that was the question. Sound familiar? Yep, we've all been there, stuck in a real financial conundrum.

This is where I come in. I'm incredibly excited to teach you all the ins and outs of handling money. Why, you ask? Because coming to grips with your green (money, not vegetables!) from a young age is like having a superpower. My mission, should you choose to accept it, is to make the maze of money matters not just simple but super fun to navigate.

This book isn't your average, dry-as-toast guide to financial literacy. Nope, it's your golden ticket to becoming a money mastermind. Through relatable scenarios and brain-tickling activities at the end of each chapter, we'll embark on an epic adventure. We'll cover it all, from the basics of budgeting, the secrets of saving, and the ins and outs of investing to the wonders of wise spending. And the best part? It's going to be a blast!

Now, before we dive headfirst into this financial fiesta, let me share a little secret with you. Once upon a time, I, too, was baffled by dollars and cents. It took a handful of mistakes and a bucket load of lessons to get where I am today, financially independent and able to buy the things I need and want. So believe me when I say I get it. And that's exactly why I'm here, ready to guide you through the twists and turns of money management.

As we journey together through the pages of this book, I encourage you to jump into the activities, ponder the discussions, and have an ah-ha moment or two. What do you say? Ready to crack the code on cash, conquer your financial fears, and have a little fun along the way? Let's do this!

Get your FREE Financial Literacy Worksheets for Kids!

Get the most out of "The Ultimate Guide to Financial Literacy for Kids" with our exclusive set of 8 FREE worksheets

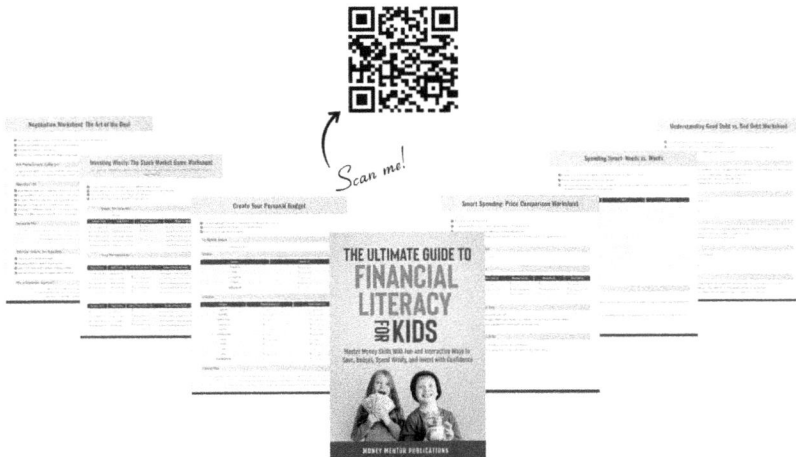

Scan me!

What's Inside:

Make Your Own Budget
Track Your Savings Goals
Identify Needs vs Wants
Play the Stock Market Game
Smart Spending Comparison Sheet
Practice Your Negotiation Skills
Differentiate between "Good Debt" and "Bad Debt"
Practice Adjusting Your Budget

CHAPTER 1
MONEY MATTERS

Have you ever considered that every time you reach for your piggy bank or wallet, you're not simply grabbing cash but holding a key to the world? Yep, you heard that right. Money isn't just paper and metal. It's a ticket to adventure, a bridge to dreams, and sometimes, a bit of a puzzle. This chapter, my friends, is where we crack the code on why money makes the world go 'round and why understanding its powers can turn you into a wizard in your own right.

1.1 WHY MONEY MATTERS: UNDERSTANDING ITS ROLE

Let's kick things off with a simple question: What is money? At first glance, it might seem like just pieces of paper or some coins that jingle in your pocket. But, oh, it's so much more. Money is a really powerful tool that humans invented to solve some pretty big headaches. Imagine trying to trade your skateboard for a new video game. How would you decide if it's a fair trade? And what if the person with the video game didn't want a skateboard? Enter money, the superhero solution to these dilemmas.

Medium of Exchange

The first superpower of money is its role as a medium of exchange. This means it can be traded for goods and services. Without money, we'd be stuck in a barter system. This means that we would need to trade something we have to get something in return. Picture trying to buy a candy bar by trading socks. Sounds tricky, right? Money simplifies this process. It's universally accepted, so you don't have to find someone who wants your specific item for trade. Instead, you hand over some cash, and voilà, that candy bar is yours. This system works because everyone agrees that money has value, making buying and selling as easy as pie.

Future Value

Next up is money's role as a storehouse of value. This means you can save it now and spend it later, and it will still hold its worth. Imagine burying a treasure chest of toys. Over time, those toys might get damaged or lose their appeal. Money, on the other hand, maintains its value over time, allowing you to plan for the future. Whether you're saving up for a new bike or stashing away birthday money for something bigger, money's ability to preserve value over time makes it possible to reach bigger goals.

Unit of Account

Money also acts as a unit of account. This is a fancy way of saying it helps us measure the value of different things in a consistent way. For instance, how do you decide if a video game is worth more than a movie ticket? Money allows us to compare the two by assigning a price to each. It's like having a universal measuring stick for value, making it easier for everyone to understand how much things are worth. This not only makes shopping easier but also helps businesses set prices and keep track of their finances.

Standard of Deferred Payment

Lastly, money serves as a standard of deferred payment. That sounds complex, but it's just a way of saying that money allows you to buy things now and pay for them later. Ever heard of a credit card? It's a tool that lets you do exactly that. You can purchase something today, and instead of paying with cash on the spot, you agree to pay the bank back in the future. This concept is crucial for big purchases, like a house or a car, where paying all at once might not be possible. It's all about trust; the seller trusts that money will hold its value over time, and you get the flexibility to manage your finances over a longer period.

So there you have it. Money isn't just pieces of paper and metal. It's a key player in our daily lives, making transactions smoother, letting us save for the future, keeping track of value, and allowing for future payments. Its roles are crucial not just in personal finance but also in the global economy. Understanding these roles gives you a solid foundation to build your financial literacy, turning you into a savvy saver, a wise spender, and an all-around money maestro.

1.2 EARNING YOUR FIRST DOUGH: HOW KIDS CAN MAKE MONEY

Gathering your own stack of cash isn't just for grown-ups with jobs. Nope, even as a kid, there are plenty of ways to get a taste of earning your own money and start filling up that piggy bank. Let's check out some cool ideas that can help you start earning and learning about the value of a dollar (or whatever currency you're into).

Allowances

First up, let's talk allowances. This is like your first dip into the world of earning. Some parents offer their kids allowances in exchange for doing chores around the house. Chores could be anything from making your bed or taking out the trash to helping with dishes. This setup is a great way to learn about responsibility and the sweet rewards that come after hard work. Plus, managing your allowance teaches you to make decisions about spending and saving. Think of it as your budget to manage every week or month.

Saving Birthday and Holiday Money

Birthdays and holidays can sometimes feel like hitting a jackpot, right? Gifts and money from family and friends start rolling in and spending it all in one go is tempting. Here's a thought: What if you saved a portion of that money instead? This is a fantastic way to boost your savings quickly. It also teaches you the value of delayed gratification—saving now for something bigger and better down the line. Maybe there's a new game, a gadget, or even a trip you've been dreaming about. Saving your gift money gets you closer to those goals, and it's an excellent practice for managing unexpected cash influxes.

Small Businesses for Kids

If you're feeling more entrepreneurial, starting a simple business could be your ticket to earning more dough. The classic lemonade stand is a great example, but don't stop there. Got a green thumb? How about offering to plant flowers or do some gardening for neighbors? Or if you're handy with a lawnmower, lawn mowing services could be in demand, especially during the summer. Neighbors don't enjoy cleaning up after their pets? Start a pooper scooper or a dog walking service. These small ventures can teach you heaps about running a business, from setting prices to marketing your services and handling your earnings. Remember, every big entrepreneur started small, and your lemonade stand or gardening service could be the beginning of something huge.

Turning Hobbies Into Income

Your hobbies are like seeds: They can grow into something more with a bit of care and creativity. Whether making jewelry, coding games, or baking cupcakes, there's a world out there eager to see what you can do. Here are a few pathways to consider:

- **Selling homemade crafts**: Kids who enjoy crafting can sell their creations, such as jewelry, keychains, or decorated notebooks, online through platforms like Etsy or eBay, at local craft fairs, or to friends and family.
- **Teaching or tutoring**: Older kids who excel in a subject or hobby, like a musical instrument, art, or coding, can offer lessons to younger kids in their community or online. And for the tech-savvy, how about teaching others how to use their gadgets or offering to set up new devices?
- **Blogging or vlogging**: Kids who are passionate about writing or making videos can start a blog or YouTube channel about their hobby. Monetization can come through ads, sponsorships, or affiliate marketing.
- **Performing arts**: Kids talented in singing, dancing, acting, or playing an instrument can perform at local events, community centers, or family gatherings to earn money.
- **Gardening and selling produce**: If gardening is their hobby, kids can sell the fruits, vegetables, or flowers they grow at local farmers' markets or directly to neighbors.
- **Digital art and design**: Kids skilled in digital art or graphic design can sell their artwork online or offer their design services for invitations, logos, or custom artwork.
- **Photography**: Budding photographers can sell their photos online through stock photography websites or offer their services for family portraits or local events.
- **Game streaming**: For kids who love video games, streaming on platforms like Twitch can eventually generate income through subscriber donations, ads, and sponsorships.

Tips for Parents

Offer guidance and support. Help your kids set up their ventures while teaching them about safety, especially online.

Marketing Your Hobby

Getting the word out there is like casting a spell; it only works if you have the right ingredients. Your passion is contagious, and with a dash of marketing, you can reach people who are just as excited about your hobby as you are. Consider these tips:

- With your parents' permission and help, use social media to showcase your work. Regular posts, engaging stories, and behind-the-scenes glimpses can attract a loyal following.
- Word of mouth is powerful. Encourage friends and family to spread the word about your products or services.
- Attend local fairs, markets, or community events where you can display your crafts, perform, or give a quick class. It's a great way to get noticed.

Earning your own money as a kid is a crash course in responsibility, hard work, and creativity. Whether through allowances, starting your own business, saving gift money, or finding unique ways to earn, each experience is packed with valuable lessons. Plus, watching your savings grow from your own efforts? That's a feeling of accomplishment money can't buy.

Success Stories

Inspiration surrounds us, with many young entrepreneurs turning their hobbies into success stories. Take, for instance, a teenager who started making candles in her kitchen and now runs a thriving online store, or a group of friends who turned their love for gaming into a popular YouTube channel that entertains and educates about coding and game design. Then there's the young artist who began sharing her drawings on social media and now sells prints and commissions worldwide.

Each story is unique, but they all share a common thread—a passion turned into a purpose, driven by creativity, hard work, and smart financial moves. These stories aren't just tales of success; they prove that with the right approach, your hobby can open doors to exciting opportunities.

Turning your hobby into a money-making venture is a mix of fun, work, and learning. It teaches you about doing what you love and sharing that love with the world while being smart about managing the financial side of things. It's a path that requires creativity, courage, and a bit of business savvy, and it's incredibly rewarding, offering lessons and experiences that go far beyond just making money. So go ahead, take that hobby of yours and see where it can lead you. Who knows? It may be the beginning of an amazing adventure.

1.3 THE CONCEPT OF EXCHANGE: MONEY FOR GOODS AND SERVICES

Imagine walking into your favorite candy store, eyes wide as you scan rows upon rows of sugary delights. You pick a chocolate bar and hand over a dollar; the treat is yours. This simple act is a classic example of an exchange. Money doesn't just sit pretty in your wallet. It's the key that unlocks the vast world of goods and services.

Basics of Buying and Selling

At its heart, buying and selling are about exchange. You offer money, and in return, you get something you want or need: a chocolate bar, a new scooter, or a haircut. This exchange is fundamental to how markets work. Businesses provide goods or services, and people like you and me use money to buy them. It's a dance that's been going on for centuries, shaping economies big and small.

What makes this dance interesting is the decision-making process. Every time you decide to buy something, you're answering basic questions. Is this chocolate bar worth my dollar? Could my money be better spent elsewhere? These decisions are influenced by several factors, including how much you value what you're buying and how much money you have to spend.

The Role of Prices

Prices are like signals in the market. They communicate the value of goods and services, guiding both buyers and sellers. But have you ever wondered how prices are set? It might seem like magic, but there's a method to the madness.

Prices often start with costs. For a product to be sold, it must first be made, which costs money. Materials, labor, even the electricity to run machines—all these costs add up, and they influence the final price of a product. But costs aren't the only factor. Remember how we talked about decisions? How much people are willing to pay for something also plays a big role in setting prices. If everyone's clamoring for the latest video game, the price might be higher because the perceived value is high.

Supply and Demand

Now, let's get into the nitty-gritty of supply and demand, two forces that drive the market like no other. Supply is how much of something is available. Demand is how much people want it. These two have a love-hate relationship. When supply is high and demand is low, prices tend to drop. Why? Because sellers want to encourage more people to buy their surplus goods. Remember when fidget spinners first came out? Everyone wanted one (high demand) so prices were high. After a while, people lost interest and stopped buying them (low demand). But there were still a lot of them on store shelves, so the price dropped to encourage people to buy them.

On the flip side, prices can skyrocket when supply is low and demand is high. Think about concert tickets to see the biggest band in the world. There are only so many seats available and everyone wants in, so tickets cost a lot.

Understanding supply and demand can make you a smarter shopper. If you notice a new product flying off the shelves and prices rising, you might decide to wait until the hype dies down and supply catches up with demand. That way, you might get a better deal.

Making Informed Choices

Making informed choices about spending your money is like being a detective. You're gathering clues, weighing evidence, and making decisions that impact your happiness and wallet. Here's how you can sharpen your detective skills:

- **Needs vs. wants**: First, determine if what you're buying is a need (essential for living) or a want (nice to have). Needs come first, but it's okay to satisfy wants if you have the budget.

- **Value for money**: Think about the value your buying brings to your life. Is it something you'll use or enjoy often? Or will it end up forgotten in a drawer somewhere? Getting good value for your money means spending money on things that add meaning to your life.
- **Comparison shopping**: Don't just buy the first thing you see. Look around, compare prices, and check out reviews. You might find the same thing for cheaper somewhere else or discover that another product offers better quality for a similar price.
- **Long-term satisfaction**: Sometimes, spending a bit more upfront can save you money in the long run. Cheap stuff might break or wear out quickly while spending a bit more could get you something that lasts longer. It's all about looking at your purchases in terms of long-term satisfaction and savings.

Whenever you exchange money for goods or services, you make decisions that affect your financial future. By understanding the basics of buying and selling, the role of prices, and the dance of supply and demand, you equip yourself with the knowledge to make informed choices. Whether it's deciding when to buy, what to spend your money on, or how to get the most bang for your buck, being a savvy consumer puts you in the driver's seat of your financial journey.

Chapter 1 Review Activity

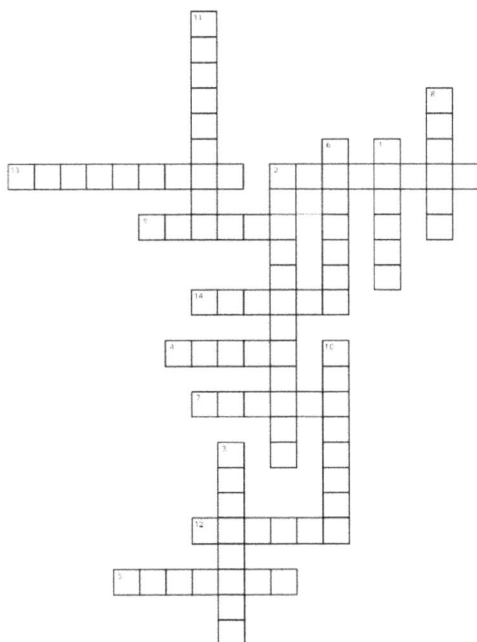

Across
2. Swapping one thing for another.
4. The importance, worth, or usefulness of something.
5. Money you keep, usually in a bank, to use later.
7. Using your money to try to make more money by buying things that could grow in value.
9. Borrowing money to buy something now and paying for it later.
12. The money you make when you sell something for more than it cost you.
13. Telling people about products or services to try to sell them.
14. How much of something is available to buy.

Down
1. Trading things you have for things you want without using money.
2. Someone who starts their own business.
3. The type of money used in a country.
6. The wealth and resources of a country or region, especially in terms of the making and selling goods and servies
8. Planning how to spend your money.
10. Extra money you pay when you borrow money or extra money you get when you save money.
11. Money given regularly, usually by parents to children.

Answer Key on Page 162

CHAPTER 2
UNLOCKING THE TREASURE CHEST: YOUR GUIDE TO SAVING WISELY

Picture this: You're on a quest, not for hidden treasure or mystic artifacts, but for something far more valuable, the secret to saving smart. In every epic tale, heroes need a trusty sidekick. In the world of finance, that sidekick is your savings strategy. It protects you against unexpected expenses, powers up your purchasing ability, and sets the stage for achieving those big, dreamy goals. So grab your financial compass, and let's navigate the seas of savings together.

2.1 PIGGY BANKS AND BEYOND: FUN WAYS TO SAVE

The journey to saving starts with finding the perfect vessel for your treasure. Think of your piggy bank not just as a container but as a companion on your financial adventure. There are all sorts of piggy banks out there. Some count your coins as you drop them in, others come in the shape of your favorite cartoon characters, and then there are digital piggy banks that connect to apps, tracking your savings with every deposit.

Selecting a piggy bank that makes you excited to save is crucial. If you're tech-savvy, a digital piggy bank might be your calling. Love something tactile? A classic ceramic piggy bank you can personalize with paint or stickers could be the way to go. Remember, the right piggy bank doesn't just hold your money, it reflects your personality and motivates you to keep adding to your stash.

Setting Savings Goals

Goals are the map that guides your saving quest. Without them, it's easy to wander off the path or lose sight of why you're saving in the first place. Start simple. You may be eyeing a new video game, planning a day out with friends, or saving for a shiny new electric scooter. Here's the trick: Write your goal on a sticky note and attach it to your piggy bank. Seeing your goal every day acts as a constant reminder and inspiration.

Tracking Progress

Visual aids are fantastic for tracking your savings progress. Create a chart or a progress bar and fill it in as your savings grow. It's like watching the loading screen on your favorite game, but this time, you're watching your financial goals come to life. Place your tracker next to your piggy bank or on your bedroom wall where you'll see it every day. Witnessing your progress can give you a real sense of accomplishment and push you to keep going.

Beyond the Piggy Bank

Once you've mastered the art of the piggy bank, it might be time to level up. Consider opening a savings account designed for kids or teens. Many banks offer accounts with no fees, teaching you the ropes of banking without the risk. With a savings account, your money isn't just sitting there. It's growing thanks to something called interest. Plus, having a bank account can make you feel like a bona fide adult, taking charge of your financial future.

Opening an account can be a family affair. Talk to your parents about helping you set one up. They can guide you through the process, from choosing the right bank to understanding how to make deposits. This step boosts your savings and teaches valuable lessons about how banks work and the importance of financial security.

Saving money is more than just hoarding coins. It's setting goals, tracking progress, and taking those first steps into the wider world of finance. Whether you're stuffing a piggy bank to its brim or managing your first bank account, every penny saved is a building block toward your financial independence. So keep feeding that piggy bank, chart your savings journey with pride, and remember, every saver starts small. Your future self will thank you for the treasures you're tucking away today.

2.2 SETTING SAVINGS GOALS: DREAMS ACHIEVED STEP BY STEP

So, you've got a piggy bank that's starting to feel like a family member, and you're ready to tackle some serious savings goals. It's like setting out on a quest to slay the dragon, except your dragon is that awesome thing you've been dreaming about. But how do you differentiate between a fleeting fancy and a genuine treasure worth pursuing? Let's dive in.

Identifying Wants and Needs

It's Saturday afternoon, and you're faced with a decision: Indulge in a giant tub of your favorite ice cream or stash away some cash for that new dirt bike. Here lies the battle between wants and needs. Wants are those sparkly, eye-catching things you can live without (yes, even that ice cream). Needs, on the other hand, are your essentials. Think of them as your quest's armor and weapons—necessary for survival.

To sort your wants from your needs, ask yourself: Will buying this help me in the long run? Or is it just for a quick happiness boost? A new bike could mean adventures with friends and a healthy hobby, while the ice cream... well, that's a fleeting pleasure. The trick is to balance between saving for needs and sprinkling in a few wants to keep the journey exciting.

When you're a kid, you might not want a lot of things. Maybe just some toys, books, and your favorite snacks. But as you get older, you'll start wanting more stuff, like cool gadgets, games, and saving for a car or college. The trick to being ready for all these wants is to start saving money now, while you don't need to spend much. Think of it like a video game, where you're collecting coins or points early on so you have plenty when the game gets tougher. Saving early gives you a big boost, like a superhero's head start, so you can handle bigger needs and wants as you grow up.

Breaking Down Goals

Why limit your dreams to the back yard when you can aim for the stars? Financial goals should be more than saving enough for a new game or a pair of sneakers. Think bigger—a college fund, your first car, or even starting your own business. These grand dreams push you to learn, grow, and think creatively about money.

SMART Goals

Setting a goal is one thing, achieving it is another. That's where SMART goals come into play. This method breaks down lofty ambitions into manageable steps:

- **Specific**: Clearly define what you want to achieve.
- **Measurable**: Set markers to track your progress.
- **Achievable**: Be realistic. It's good to stretch your abilities but stay within the realm of possibility.
- **Relevant**: Make sure the goal matters to you. There's no point working toward something you're not passionate about.
- **Time-bound**: Set a deadline. A goal without a timeline is just a wish.

For example, instead of saying, "I just want to save money," a SMART goal would be, "I will save $300 for a new bike by saving $25 from my allowance each month for the next 12 months."

Visualizing Success

Have you ever heard of athletes visualizing their wins? It works for financial goals, too. Creating a vision board can bring your goals to life. Grab a poster board or use a digital app and start collecting images that represent your financial aspirations. Place it somewhere you'll see daily. This constant visual reminder keeps your goals front and center, fueling your motivation to make them a reality.

Involving Family and Friends

Sharing your goals can turn them into a group effort. Your family could offer to match what you save dollar for dollar, or a friend will jump on board with a similar goal, turning it into a friendly competition. Talking about your goals makes it easier to stick to them and get help, and helps you feel less alone and more likely to succeed.

Setting ambitious goals is the first step in a larger adventure. It's about aiming high, crafting a plan, and taking consistent action toward making those dreams a reality. With SMART goals, visualization techniques, and the support of your crew, you're not just dreaming big, you're setting the sails for a successful financial journey.

Making Saving a Game

Who said saving money can't be a blast? Introducing gamification to your savings strategy can transform it from a chore into a challenge you're eager to beat. Set up a savings challenge with your friends or family—see who can save the most money in a month by cutting back on non-essentials. Or create a personal savings bingo card with squares for different saving tasks: "No Spend Day," "Do an Extra

Chore," "Save All Money Earned." Celebrate victories with non-monetary rewards, like an at-home movie night.

Leveraging Technology

In today's digital age, your smartphone (or your parent's phone) is your magic wand for savings. Financial apps can track your spending, round up purchases to save the difference, and even invest spare change. But let's not stop there. Use technology to compare prices in real time with barcode scanning apps, ensuring you always get the best deal. And for the wizards in training, setting up alerts for price drops on wanted items can mean big savings with minimal effort.

- With your parent's help, download budgeting apps to keep your spending in check.
- Use price comparison apps when shopping to always ensure the best deal.
- Set up price drop alerts for items on your wishlist.

DIY and Upcycling

The old becomes new with a flick of your wrist, or rather, with a bit of creativity and elbow grease. Before you throw something out or rush to buy new, ask yourself if it can be repurposed or fixed. Jars can turn into stylish organizers, old game pieces can be used to create a brand-new game. The internet is a treasure trove of do-it-yourself tutorials for just about anything. Not only does reusing save money, but it also reduces waste—a double win.

- Turn scrap fabric into bags, pillow covers, or even art supplies.
- Turn old bottles into vases or create wall art from magazine cutouts.

- Fix, rather than replace. Often, a simple YouTube tutorial is all you need to repair something.

Adjusting as You Grow

Your goals are living, breathing aspirations that evolve as you do. The financial target you set at the beginning of the year might not make sense six months down the line, and that's okay. Regularly looking at your goals allows you to tweak them, ensuring they still align with what's important to you. It's like updating a game; as you level up, your objectives might change, requiring new strategies and tools.

2.3 CELEBRATING MILESTONES: REWARDS ALONG THE WAY

Imagine reaching the top of a mountain after a long hike. You're out of breath, your legs are tired, but the view and the sense of accomplishment are unmatched. We aim for this feeling as we navigate our financial goals. Every milestone reached is like a checkpoint in our adventure, deserving its own moment of recognition and celebration. Here's how we can make these moments count and keep our spirits high without losing sight of the bigger picture.

Designing Rewards

Crafting a reward system is like planting little treasures along your path, encouraging you to keep moving forward. Plan a reward for every financial milestone that matches the effort it took to get there. If you've saved half of your target for that iPad you've been eyeing, why not treat yourself to a day out at your favorite park? The trick is to ensure these rewards stay within your savings plan. They should be thoughtful yet modest—reminders of your progress that spur you on rather than set you back. List your milestones for a particular goal. Next to each, jot down a reward that feels appropriate. This list is your roadmap. It keeps you aware of the next celebration and motivates you to reach your goal.

Milestone Celebration Ideas:

- **Homemade trophy for "Saver of the Month"**: Craft a unique trophy using recycled materials to celebrate the family member who saved the most that month.
- **Special Family Game Night**: Use a small part of the savings to buy a new board game for the family to enjoy together, celebrating your financial achievement.
- **DIY Certificate of Achievement**: Create personalized certificates for each family member when they hit their savings goal, complete with fun titles and decorations.
- **Savings Goal Chart Party**: When the family savings chart

is filled, have a party with homemade snacks or a movie night at home.

- **Picnic in the park**: Pack a picnic with everyone's favorite homemade treats and head to the park to celebrate reaching a savings milestone.
- **Craft a savings scrapbook**: Start a scrapbook documenting your financial journey, adding photos, notes, and milestones achieved along the way.
- **Financial freedom jar**: Each time someone reaches a goal, they get to add a colorful marble or stone to a communal jar, visually showcasing your collective achievements.
- **Savings jars decorating contest**: Have a contest to decorate individual savings jars using a variety of craft supplies, and celebrate with a small prize for the most creative jar.
- **Write a family newsletter**: Include updates on your financial goals, achievements, and fun facts or jokes. Share it with family and friends to celebrate your progress.
- **Host a "Future Dreams" dinner**: Prepare a special meal at home where each family member shares their dreams for the future, funded by your ongoing savings.
- **Build a goal tracker wall**: Designate a wall or board in the house to track savings goals with colorful post-its or magnets. Celebrate when you need to add a new goal because the previous one was achieved.
- **Create a savings song or chant**: Collaborate on a fun song or chant about saving money and perform it together when you reach a milestone.
- **Plant a garden**: Dedicate a new plant or flower to each financial milestone achieved, creating a thriving garden of your accomplishments.
- **Memory box for receipts and notes**: Start a memory box where you keep receipts or notes related to your

financial goals, adding a new item each time a goal is reached.

- **Financial goals vision board party**: When major milestones are hit, host a vision board party where each person creates a board depicting their future goals, fueled by financial success.

Balancing Rewards and Savings

The art of rewarding yourself while continuing to save is a delicate balance. You must find joy in the now while keeping your future goals in focus. One approach is to set aside a small percentage of what you save for your reward fund. For example, for every $100 saved, $5 goes into a separate "reward pot." This method keeps your primary savings intact while giving you something to look forward to. It's a win-win that celebrates your dedication without compromising your end goal.

Set Clear Boundaries

Decide on the percentage of your savings that will go toward rewards. Stick to this rule to keep things consistent and fair to both your present and your future self.

Non-Monetary Rewards

Rewards don't have to cost money. In fact, some of the most meaningful celebrations involve experiences or privileges rather than material goods. For small wins, you might get an extra hour of screen time on the weekend or you get to choose the family movie night film. Larger achievements could be marked by a day dedicated to your favorite activities, all chosen by you. These kinds of rewards enrich your life with experiences, not things, and they remind you that the journey toward your financial goals can be fun and fulfilling.

Creativity Is Key

Think outside the box for ways to celebrate that don't involve spending. There may be a skill you've wanted to learn, and now's the perfect time to start. Use your milestones as opportunities to enrich your life in diverse ways.

Reflecting on Achievements

Taking the time to reflect on what you've accomplished is crucial. You're not just patting yourself on the back, you're witnessing how each milestone brings you closer to your larger goals. Set aside some time after reaching a milestone to write down how you achieved it, what challenges you faced, and how you overcame those challenges. This reflection turns your achievements into learning experiences, giving you insights and strategies to apply to future goals. It transforms each milestone from a mere checkpoint into a stepping stone, paving your way to success.

Keep a Journal

Dedicate a section of your financial journal to reflections. After each milestone, fill in a new entry. Over time, this section will become a testament to your growth and a guidebook filled with personal wisdom.

2.4 THE POWER OF PATIENCE: WAITING FOR WHAT YOU WANT

Now, let's talk about the golden virtue of saving: patience. It's not just waiting; it's believing in the magic of tomorrow. Consider the story of Mia. Mia saved her allowance for a whole year to buy a professional-grade telescope. There were times when dazzling video games and trendy clothes tempted her, but Mia kept her eyes on the stars—literally. When she finally gazed through her new telescope, the stars weren't just bright, they were her reward for patience.

Patience teaches us that some dreams are worth the wait. It turns saving into an adventure rather than a chore. Every time you choose to save instead of spend, you're one step closer to your goal. It's not easy, especially when shiny temptations pop up, but remember Mia and her stars. Your telescope moment is just around the corner.

Delayed Gratification

Delayed gratification is a fancy term for waiting for the good stuff. It means choosing to hold off on smaller, immediate rewards so you can earn bigger, more fulfilling rewards down the line. Think of it like this: You could spend your allowance on a bunch of small toys now, or you could save up for that mega Lego set you've been eyeing for months. Choosing the latter is a classic case of delayed gratification. Delayed gratification isn't just about saving money. It trains your brain to seek long-term happiness and satisfaction.

Success Stories

Let's talk about Sam. Sam had his eye on a top-of-the-line gaming console. It was a big goal, especially for a kid. Instead of splurging on smaller items, Sam decided to save every penny he could. Birthdays, holidays, even doing extra chores for neighbors—every bit of money went into his savings. It took over a year, but the day Sam walked into the store and bought his console with his own money was unforgettable. That console was more than just a gaming device; it was a trophy, a reminder of his patience and determination.

Then there's Lucy. Lucy dreamed of going to a summer camp known for its amazing outdoor adventures. The catch? It was pretty pricey. Lucy got creative. She started her own business selling handmade bracelets. It was slow going at first, but she kept at it, saving every sale's proceeds. When summer rolled around, Lucy had enough to cover camp fees. The experience was incredible, packed with memories and friendships that would last a lifetime.

Activities to Build Patience

Building patience, especially when saving money, can be fun. Here are a few activities to try:

- **The savings calendar**: Create a colorful calendar dedicated to your savings goal. Add a sticker or stamp for each week or month you add money to your savings. Watching your calendar fill up over time is satisfying and visually reminds you of your progress.
- **The patience jar**: Get two jars and fill one with marbles or beads, each representing a portion of your savings goal. Each time you add money to your savings, move a marble to the other jar. Watching the second jar fill up is surprisingly motivating and makes the concept of saving more tangible.
- **Goal visualization**: Spend some time drawing or crafting a representation of your goal. It could be a poster of that bike you're saving for or a camera you want. Place it where you'll see it every day. This visual reminder of what you're working toward can help keep your focus on the long-term prize.

Relating Patience to Saving

Patience and saving money are like two peas in a pod. They go hand in hand, each strengthening the other. When you save, you're practicing patience, waiting for something you want rather than going for instant gratification. And as you become more patient, saving becomes easier. You start to see the bigger picture, understanding that some things are worth the wait.

Saving with patience also teaches valuable life lessons beyond just financial smarts. It builds character, teaching resilience, determination, and the ability to set and achieve goals. These skills are like superpowers, equipping you to tackle financial challenges and any obstacle life throws your way.

So take a moment next time you find yourself itching to spend your savings on something small. Think about your bigger goal, the one that requires a bit of waiting and a bit of patience. Remember, the most rewarding treasures are often those we wait for, those we save for, step by step, day by day.

2.5 FROM PENNIES TO DOLLARS: WATCHING YOUR SAVINGS GROW

Imagine your savings as a tiny seed you've just planted in the ground. At first, it doesn't look like much, but give it time, water, and care, and one day it'll sprout into a flourishing tree. In the world of savings, "interest" is the water and care that helps your money-seed grow. Banks offer interest as a thank-you for keeping your money with them. It's like they're renting the money from you and paying you rent in return. And the best part? You don't have to do anything extra! Your money grows all on its own.

Interest Explained

When you save money in a bank, the bank uses your money to lend to others. In return, they add interest, a percentage of your savings, to your account. It's a win-win. You get extra money just for saving, and the bank gets to use your funds for its operations. Think of interest as a reward for being patient and savvy with your savings.

Compound Interest

Now, let's talk about a real game-changer: compound interest. It's interest on top of interest. Imagine you save $100, and your bank offers you 10% interest annually. After the first year, you have $110. In the second year, you earn interest not just on your original $100 but also on the $10 interest from the first year. By the end of the second year, you have $121. This cycle continues, and over time, your savings balloon not just from your deposits but from the accumulating interest. Compound interest is like a snowball rolling down a big hill, gathering more snow, and getting bigger with each turn.

Real-World Examples

Let's meet Jamie and Taylor, two friends passionate about saving. Jamie started saving $20 every month from age 10, while Taylor waited until turning 15 to start saving the same amount. They both chose savings accounts with an interest rate that capitalized on the magic of compounding. By the time they were 25, Taylor had a respectable sum of $3,461.70, but Jamie, who started earlier, had significantly more at $6,339.25—all thanks to the head start and the power of compound interest.

As we wrap up this chapter, remember that every penny you save today is a step toward a brighter, more secure tomorrow. Watching your savings grow from pennies to dollars, thanks to the wonders of interest and compound interest, proves that even the smallest amount set aside can transform into significant savings. Play the long game, where patience, consistency, and time are your best allies. As we move forward, we'll explore how to make smart moves with the money you've grown, ensuring it continues to work for you and paving the way for a future filled with possibilities.

Chapter 2 Review Activity

V	I	S	I	O	N	B	O	A	R	D	U	G	T	K	J
C	Z	S	Y	K	F	E	J	N	Q	Y	P	M	N	Z	G
H	O	T	G	K	D	N	S	X	A	C	C	O	U	N	T
A	W	M	C	M	O	S	B	X	D	J	Y	Y	G	U	L
L	I	Q	P	H	K	P	A	I	I	R	C	N	N	D	N
L	E	V	X	O	S	R	E	V	G	Q	L	D	B	N	S
E	B	D	D	P	U	A	E	I	I	Y	I	Y	P	L	S
N	O	L	M	I	I	N	M	W	T	N	N	Y	A	X	S
G	N	J	V	W	N	G	D	E	A	I	G	O	T	W	C
E	B	C	B	E	H	T	G	I	L	R	G	S	I	T	K
P	T	U	S	C	Q	D	E	Y	N	O	D	M	E	W	U
G	R	Z	A	O	U	Y	V	R	B	G	H	G	N	X	X
Q	R	U	O	B	C	A	P	K	E	A	U	W	C	A	N
X	Z	E	G	G	C	T	C	M	C	S	N	C	E	B	T
U	I	D	H	P	G	U	X	O	F	I	T	K	U	N	R
F	O	H	T	C	R	C	M	E	K	X	E	J	Z	K	A

PiggyBank   Interest   Compounding
Challenge   Upcycling   Savings
Budget   Digital   Account
Patience   Goals   Reward
Visionboard

Answer Key on Page 162

CHAPTER 3
THE SMART SPENDER'S PLAYBOOK

Imagine you're at a carnival. Lights flashing, music blaring, and every game booth promises a chance at the grand prize. But here's the catch: You've only got a limited number of tickets to spend. Where do you use them? On the flashy, high-stakes games that catch your eye first? Or do you strategize, choosing the games that offer the best chance of winning or that you'll enjoy the most? This carnival is a lot like life's financial decisions. Every choice costs something. Making smart choices means knowing the difference between what you need and what you want, then acting wisely.

3.1 NEEDS VS. WANTS: MAKING SMART CHOICES

Defining Needs and Wants

Let's break it down. Needs are the essentials, the nonnegotiables: food, shelter, clothing (the basics, not a designer wardrobe), and maybe your education costs. Wants, on the other hand, are all the extras. They're the sprinkle on your ice cream, the neon lights on your bike, or that video game that's just been released. The tricky part? Sometimes, what we think we need is actually a want in clever disguise. Recognizing the difference is step one to smart spending.

Prioritizing Spending

Once you've separated your needs from your wants, it's time to play financial Tetris. Your budget is the game board, and you've got to fit in your needs first. The space that's left—that's where your wants come in. If there's room, great! If not, it's time to reassess and maybe decide which wants can wait. This doesn't mean cutting out fun. It just lets you make sure you've got your bases covered before adding on the extras.

The Envelope System

Here's a tactile way to manage your spending: the envelope system. Grab some envelopes and label each with a category like Food, Savings, Fun Money, you get the gist. Every time you get some cash, divide it among the envelopes based on your priorities. It's a visual and physical way to see how much money you have and make you stop spending when an envelope's empty. No more guessing if you can afford that comic book or if you should save a bit more.

Real-Life Decision Making

Now imagine you're at the store with money in your pocket. You spot a cool gadget you've been eyeing, but you also remember you're saving up for a camp next summer. Here's where you pause and think. Ask yourself, "Do I need this right now? Can it wait? What's more important in the long run?" Sometimes taking a moment to consider your options leads to smarter decisions. And hey, if you decide to wait, that gadget might be on sale by the time you've saved enough for it and the camp.

Making smart choices with your money doesn't mean you never get what you want. It means making sure you've got what you need first, then using your spending power wisely on the wants that truly matter to you. You're putting yourself in control, not letting impulse decisions lead the way. With practice, you'll find your balance. You'll become a savvy saver and a smart spender.

3.2 THE ART OF BUDGETING: PLANNING YOUR SPENDING

Picture this: You've got your own economy running. Money comes in, money goes out, and you're the boss in charge of it all. Sounds cool, right? But even bosses need a plan to make sure they're heading in the right direction. That's where a budget comes in. It's not just a list or a chart. It's your game plan for winning at money management. Let's break it down into steps and skills that'll make you a budgeting pro before you even realize it.

What Is a Budget?

Think of a budget as your personal finance map. It shows you what you're earning, what you're spending, and where you can save. It's like having a financial snapshot that helps you make decisions about your cash flow. Why bother? Well, with a budget, you can see if you're spending too much on video games and not enough on saving for that cool skateboard. It helps you set your spending limits and shows you where your money's going every month.

Creating a Simple Budget

All right, ready to set up your own budget? Here's a simple way to start:

1. **Track your money**: Write down everything you spend money on, no matter how much, for one week (or one month). Those candies and online game credits add up.
2. **Income vs. expenses**: List your income sources (allowance, chore money, birthday money, etc.) and your expenses (things you spend money on). Use your one-week track as a guide for your monthly expenses.
3. **Set categories**: Divide your expenses into categories like Needs, Wants, and Savings. It'll help you see where your money's going.
4. **Allocate funds**: Decide how much money goes into each category. As a kid who doesn't pay for a lot of your needs yet, you could decide to put 50% in savings and spend 30% on wants and 20% on needs. As you grow older, these percentages will change. You'll also make adjustments based on what you learn from tracking your spending.
5. **Tools**: Use a simple spreadsheet, a budgeting app, or good old paper and pencil to keep it organized.

Sticking to a budget

Sticking to a budget might sound tough, but making it a habit is worth the effort. Here are some ways to stay on track:

- **Weekly check-ins**: Once a week, take a few minutes to review your budget. It'll help you catch any overspending early, before you get off track.

- **Fun money**: Always include a category for Fun Money. This is money you can spend however you like, guilt-free. Knowing you have this can make sticking to the other parts of your budget easier.
- **Visual reminders**: Put a chart or a picture of what you're saving for in a place where you'll see it every day. It'll remind you why sticking to your budget is worth it.
- **Accountability buddy**: Team up with a friend or family member and share your budgeting goals. Sticking to a plan is easier when you know someone's rooting for you.

Adjusting Your Budget

Your budget isn't set in stone. Life changes and your budget should, too. Here's when and how to tweak it:

- **Regular reviews**: At the end of each month, compare your planned budget with what you actually spent. Look for patterns. You may be consistently overspending in one area or allocating too much to another.
- **Life changes**: Got a bump in your allowance? Or maybe there's a new expense on the horizon? Adjust your budget to reflect these changes.
- **Goal shifts**: If your financial goals change (say, now you're saving for a computer instead of a hoverboard), update your budget to match your new priorities.
- **Trial and error**: Feel free to experiment with your budget. You may prefer saving a little more for wants and a little less for needs. Adjust, try it out, and see how it goes.

Creating and sticking to a budget is a dynamic process. Find what works for you and tweak it as you go. With each adjustment, you'll learn more about your spending habits and how to manage your money better. Remember, the goal isn't to restrict your spending but to empower you to make smart choices with your money. With a solid budget, you're not just planning your spending—you're planning for success.

3.3 WISE SHOPPER TACTICS: GETTING MORE BANG FOR YOUR BUCK

So, you've got your eyes on the prize—that epic gadget that's been calling your name. But wait! Before you hand over your hard-earned cash, let's put on our detective hats and dig into some tactics that ensure you're not just spending wisely but you're also getting the most bang for your buck.

Comparing Prices

In the internet age, finding the best deal is like a treasure hunt—exciting, rewarding, and sometimes challenging. Here's the scoop: Always check different stores (both online and in person) for the price of the item you want. Apps and websites can scan a broad range of retailers to show you where to find the best deal. Sometimes, the price difference can be eye-opening. It might mean waiting a bit longer for shipping or a trip to a different store, but the savings can be worth the extra effort. (See Chapter 10.3 for a list of helpful websites and apps.)

- Tip: Use price comparison tools or apps. They do the heavy lifting by comparing prices across multiple sites in real-time.
- Exercise: Next time you're shopping, pick an item and compare its price in at least three different places. Note the differences and where you find the best deal.

Understanding Value

Here's a little secret: The best deal isn't always the cheapest option. Shocking, right? But think about it—value is about more than just the price tag. It's about what you're getting for your money. A toy might be cheaper at one store, but if it's a lower-quality version that'll break in a week, is it really worth it? Assessing value means looking at durability, warranty, and how much use you'll get out of it. Sometimes, paying a bit more upfront for something that lasts longer or provides more enjoyment is the smarter move.

Reflection

Think of something you bought because it was cheap then later regretted buying it. Now, think of a purchase that was a bit more expensive, but you felt it was worth every penny. What made the difference?

Coupons and Sales

Coupons and sales are like the secret codes of shopping. They can unlock deals and discounts that make your money stretch further. Here's how you can become a coupon whiz:

- Keep an eye on sales cycles. Many stores have predictable patterns for marking down items or offering special sales. After the holidays is a common time for big discounts.
- With your parents' permission and help, sign up for newsletters and loyalty programs. Your inbox might get a bit fuller, but you'll be in the loop for exclusive coupons and sale alerts.
- Use coupon apps and websites. They compile current coupons and promo codes in one place, making it easy to

find discounts for the stores you love. Make sure your parents are okay with the site before you use it.

- Create a coupon organizer. It can be a simple folder or a digital document where you keep track of coupons, sale dates, and promo codes. Make a habit of checking it before making a purchase.

Quality vs. Quantity

There's an age-old debate: Is it better to have many things that might not last or a few really good items? Here's a thought—investing in quality means you buy less often because your stuff doesn't wear out as quickly. It's like choosing between a cheap pair of shoes that fall apart after a few months and a more expensive pair that lasts for years. In the long run, the pricier pair is actually the better deal. Plus, it's kinder to our planet. Less waste, less clutter, and more value for you.

Consider Alex's experience. He decided to buy a high-quality backpack instead of the cheaper option. While his friends were on their third or fourth backpacks two years later, Alex's was still going strong, looking as good as new. The initial price was higher, but the cost per use was much lower.

Navigating the world of smart shopping is more than just finding the lowest price. When you become a savvy spender, you know how to compare prices, assess the true value of a product, take advantage of sales and coupons, and choose quality over quantity. With these tactics in your toolkit, you're investing your money in a way that brings you the most joy, use, and satisfaction. Remember, every smart purchase is a step toward becoming a more empowered, informed, and wise consumer.

3.4 AVOIDING IMPULSE BUYS: THINK BEFORE YOU SPEND

Have you ever walked past a store where a shiny new gadget caught your eye, whispering sweet nothings like, "Buy me now!" into your brain? That, my friends, is the siren call of an impulse buy. It's that thing you didn't know you "needed" until you saw it, and now, suddenly, you can't imagine life without it. But here's the kicker: More often than not, these purchases end up forgotten, gathering dust, or worse, causing a twinge of regret. Let's navigate this tricky terrain with some smart strategies.

What are Impulse Buys?

Impulse purchases are like those sneaky snack attacks. They happen fast, driven by emotion rather than need or planning. One minute, you're fine, and the next, you're itching to spend on something that wasn't even on your radar. These buys can be problematic because they munch away at your budget, leaving less for what you're saving up for.

The 24-hour Rule

Here's a nifty trick to combat those impulsive urges: the 24-hour rule. It's simple. When you feel the pull toward an unplanned purchase, pause and give yourself a full day to think it over. This brief break allows the initial "gotta have it" rush to fade, giving you time to consider whether you really want or need the item. You'll often find that the urge diminishes or that the item wasn't as essential as it seemed just yesterday.

Set Spending Limits

Another way to keep impulse buys in check is by setting clear spending limits for different categories of purchases. This means deciding on a specific amount you're comfortable spending on things like entertainment, clothes, or eating out each month. Once you hit that limit, spending is a no-go zone until the next month rolls around. This boundary helps you stay mindful of your spending and keeps your budget on track.

- Break your budget down into categories.
- Assign a monthly spending limit to each category.
- Stick to these limits, and if a category runs dry, wait until you refill it before buying anything else.

Reflection and Regret

Ever bought something on a whim and then wondered, "Why did I even get this?" You're not alone. Reflecting on past impulse purchases can be a powerful way to learn and grow. Take time to think about purchases you regret, how they made you feel afterward, and what you could have done differently. Don't reflect just to beat yourself up. Learn from the past so you can make smarter choices in the future.

- Keep a small journal or list of purchases you regret and why you regret them.
- Review this list when you're tempted to make an impulse buy.

By understanding the nature of impulse buys, employing the 24-hour rule, setting firm spending limits, and reflecting on past regrets, you'll equip yourself with a robust toolkit to combat those spur-of-the-moment spending urges. You'll become more intentional with your money, ensuring each purchase adds real value to your life.

As we wrap up this exploration into smart spending tactics, remember that the power lies in your hands (or wallet). The strategies we've discussed are tools to help you make choices that align with your goals, values, and financial well-being. Heading into the next chapter, we'll pivot from saving and spending to the exciting world of making your money grow. Think of it as moving from defense to offense in the game of financial literacy. Ready to level up?

Chapter 3 Review Activity

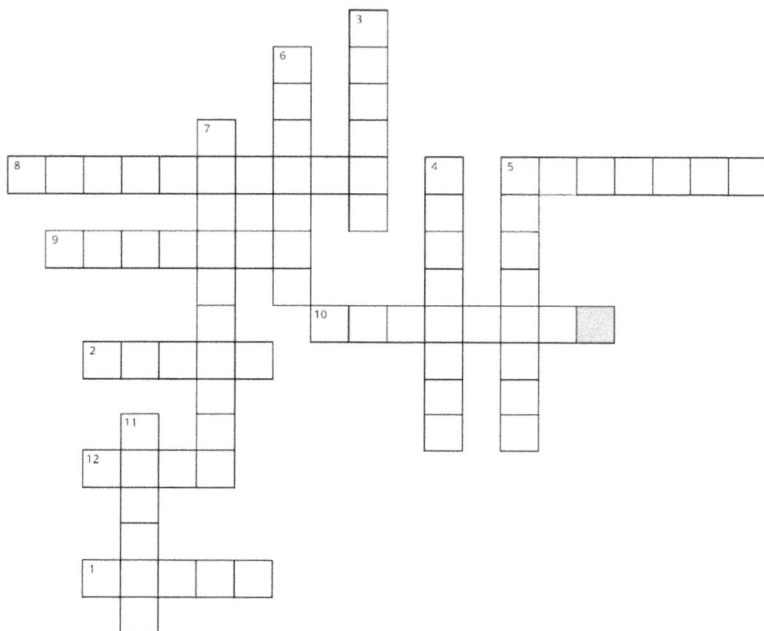

Across

1. Things you must have to live and be safe, like food, a place to live, and clothes (but not the fancy kind).
2. All the extra fun stuff you like, such as toys, games, or treats, but don't really need to live.
5. Money set aside for future use or emergencies.
8. A cool trick where you wait a whole day before buying something you suddenly want, to see if you still really want it later.
9. Special tickets that let you buy stuff for less money, like getting a dollar off your favorite ice cream.
10. How good or sturdy something is. Sometimes, spending more on something that lasts longer is smarter than buying the cheapest option.
12. When stores lower prices on items for a short time, so you can get things you need or want for less money.

Down

3. It's like a plan for how to spend your allowance or birthday money so you can buy things you need, save some, and still have fun.
4. A method of dividing cash into categories for spending and saving.
5. Planning and tactics used to manage financial resources effectively.
6. Buying something suddenly without thinking it through, like grabbing a candy bar while waiting in line at the store.
7. The action of arranging or dealing with something according to its importance.
11. A small cool tool or device, often something new and fun, like a smartphone or a video game console.

Answer Key on Page 162

CHAPTER 4
MAKING YOUR MONEY GROW: THE BEGINNER'S GUIDE TO INVESTING

W hy do some people seem to have a magic touch when it comes to money? It's like they've got a green thumb, but instead of growing epic tomatoes, they're growing their cash. Here's the secret: It's not magic, it's investing. Think of investing as planting your money seeds in different pots and watching them sprout and bloom into a lush garden. Intrigued? Let's dig into the soil of investing and uncover how you can start growing your financial garden today.

4.1 WHAT IS INVESTING? MONEY MAKING MONEY

Investing is like leveling up in a video game. Instead of keeping your money under the mattress (or in a savings account where it slowly grows), you put it out into the world where it can work harder for you. When you invest, you buy things you believe will increase in value over time. These could be pieces of a company (stocks), loans you give out (bonds), or even a savings account that pays you interest.

The goal? To make your initial pile of money bigger without having to mow more lawns or babysit more kids.

Types of Investments

Let's break down your investment options:

- **Stocks**: Buying a stock means you own a tiny slice of a company. If the company does well, your slice becomes more valuable. Imagine owning a piece of your favorite video game company and getting a share of their profits!
- **Bonds**: These are like IOUs from the government or companies. You lend them money, and they promise to pay you back with a little extra added on. It's as if you're the bank, and they're taking a loan from you.
- **Savings accounts**: Not all investments require buying stocks or bonds. A high-yield savings account also counts. It's a cozy, low-risk spot for your money to grow bit by bit.

Risk vs. Reward

This is a crucial piece of the puzzle: the risk vs. reward balance. Investing can be a bit of a roller coaster. Stocks might offer big rewards, but they also come with the risk of losing value. Bonds are usually steadier, but they grow slower. It's like choosing between a wild, unpredictable game with high scores and the possibility of losing points, or a slower, more predictable one where you steadily accumulate points. The key is finding the right mixture that matches your comfort with risk and your dreams for the future.

The Long-Term Perspective

Investing is a marathon, not a sprint. You play the long game, letting your money grow over years, even decades. Think of a tree growing from a sapling to a giant oak. It doesn't happen overnight. That's how investing works. It takes patience and time, but the rewards can be worth it. You're not just saving for something a year from now. You're building wealth that can support your dreams far into the future.

Investing your money is an exciting step toward financial independence. By understanding the basics, like the different types of investments and the balance between risk and reward, you're laying down the foundation for a prosperous future. You're making your money work for you, growing your financial garden one investment at a time. So grab your financial tools, and let's start planting those money seeds.

4.2 SIMPLE INVESTMENT OPTIONS FOR KIDS

When you think about investing, you might picture people in suits furiously trading stocks on Wall Street. But guess what? Even as a kid, you have some cool options to start growing your own pot of gold. Let's peel back the curtain on some investment choices that are kid-friendly and great learning opportunities.

Savings Accounts With Interest

You know that piggy bank sitting on your shelf? Imagine if, every month, it magically had a little more money in it just because you'd been keeping your savings there. That's how a savings account with interest works. Banks reward you for letting them hold onto your money by paying you interest, a percentage of your savings. Here's why it's a solid first step into the world of investing:

- **Safety:** Your money is super safe in a bank. Even if the bank were to run into trouble, insurance covers your cash up to a certain amount.
- **Easy access**: Need to dip into your savings? No problem. You can get to your money easily, which is great for unexpected expenses or when you've finally saved enough for that big purchase.
- **Learning to save**: Watching your balance grow with interest can be a big motivator to save more. It's like getting paid just for being smart with your money.

Certificates of Deposit (CDs)

Think of CDs as a special ticket you buy for a money-growing ride. When you get a certificate of deposit, you tell the bank, "Hey, you can use my money for a bit." In return, they promise to pay you more interest than a regular savings account. The catch? You agree not to touch your money for a certain period, like six months or a year. Here are some reasons why CDs can be awesome:

- **Higher interest rates**: Because you agree to leave your money alone for a while, banks pay you more interest.
- **Time choices**: You can pick how long you want to lock in your money based on how long you think you can wait.
- **Safe and predictable**: CDs are a safe bet. You know exactly how much money you'll have at the end, no surprises.

Stock Market Basics

Owning a piece of a company might sound like big business, but it's actually something kids can do, too. When you buy stocks, you get a small part of a company. If the company does well, your piece of the pie could become more valuable. Here's the scoop:

- **Ownership**: Buying stock means you own a tiny fraction of that company. You're like a mini-business owner.
- **Potential for growth**: If the company grows, so does the value of your stock. Some people have made their money grow a lot by picking the right stocks.
- **Learning opportunity**: Following your stocks can teach you loads about businesses, how they make money, and what makes them grow.

Investment Apps for Beginners

In today's digital world, there are apps for just about everything, including investing. Some super-cool apps are designed just for beginners and even allow you to practice investing without using real money. This way, you can get a feel for how investing works without any risk. Why these apps rock:

- **Simulated investing**: Many apps offer a simulated investing experience, giving you play money to invest in real stocks and see how they do.
- **Educational tools**: These apps are packed with tutorials, articles, and quizzes to help you learn the ropes of investing.
- **Real-life practice**: By using a simulated environment, you can practice buying and selling stocks, all based on real market data, which is cool for getting your feet wet in the investing world.

Diving into investing might seem like jumping into the deep end, but with these kid-friendly options, you're actually wading into the shallows where it's safe to learn and grow your money. From the steady climb of interest in savings accounts and CDs to the exciting world of stocks and simulated investing apps, there's a whole landscape of opportunities out there. Who knew you could have this much fun watching your money grow?

4.3 RISKS AND REWARDS: THE INVESTMENT SCALE

Investing your allowance or birthday money is different from buying a new video game or skateboard. When you decide to invest, you're stepping onto a seesaw of risks and rewards. These seesaw tips are based on the choices you make, and understanding how to balance them is part of becoming a smart investor.

Understanding Volatility

First off, volatility is a big word that often pops up when talking about investing. Simply put, it means the price of your investment can jump up and down like a kangaroo on a trampoline. One day, your investment in a cool tech company might be up, making you feel like a millionaire, and the next day, it could drop, making your heart sink.

Why does this happen? Because lots of things affect investment prices, like how well the company is doing, changes in the economy, or even news stories. Imagine if a video game company announces a hot new game release. People get excited and want to buy more stock, and the price goes up. But if something goes wrong, say, a glitch in the game that delays the launch, the price might go down.

Diversification

To avoid putting too much stress on our seesaw with volatility, we use a strategy called diversification. This might sound complicated, but it's just a fancy way of saying, "Don't put all your eggs in one basket." If you only invest in one thing, like a single stock or bond, and it takes a nosedive, you could lose a lot. But if you spread your money out over different types of investments, you're less likely to feel a big hit if one doesn't do well.

Think of it like this: Instead of saving up for that one big, expensive video game, you also pick up a couple of smaller, cheaper games. If the big game turns out to be a dud, you're not as bummed because you've got other games to enjoy. It's the same with investing. Having a mix—some stocks, some bonds, maybe a bit in a savings account— can keep your money growing steadily, even if one investment doesn't perform as expected.

Researching Before Investing

Before diving into any investment, doing your homework is key. This means spending time looking into what you're thinking about putting your money into. It's a bit like when you're eyeing that next big game purchase. You read reviews, watch gameplay videos, and even check out what other gamers are saying online.

With investing, it's similar. You'd look at how the investment has done in the past, what experts are saying about its future, and any news that might affect its performance. It's important because the more you know, the better choices you'll make. Sure, it takes a bit more time, but it's worth it to help your money grow and avoid any surprise drops in your investment's value.

The Role of Patience

Lastly, let's talk about patience—again. If investing had a best friend, patience would be it. Making your money grow through investing won't be a quick path to becoming rich. You'll have to set your sights on the horizon and wait for your investments to mature over time.

Here's the thing: Markets go up and down. That's just what they do. But over the long term, they tend to go up more than they go down. That means if you're patient and stick with your investments, and don't panic when things look a little rocky, there's a good chance your money will grow.

So remember, investing is more like growing a tree than zapping a video game boss. Trees take time to grow tall and strong, and so does your investment. The trick is to water it (with regular contributions), protect it from pests (by not making hasty decisions when the market dips), and give it time to grow. You'll see your money garden flourish with patience, turning those initial seeds into a lush canopy of financial well-being.

In the end, balancing the seesaw of risks and rewards in investing is a skill that grows with you. The more you understand volatility, the importance of diversification, the power of research, and the value of patience, the more equipped you'll be to make your money work hard for you. And while investing comes with its ups and downs, embracing these concepts will help you navigate the path to financial growth with confidence and savvy.

4.4 FUTURE FINANCIAL HEROES: KID INVESTORS' STORIES

In a world where kids are making big waves, let's spotlight some young investors who've turned their pocket money into impressive portfolios. These tales are blueprints for budding financial geniuses everywhere. Each narrative brings to life the ups and downs of investing from a kid's perspective, offering invaluable insights and inspiration.

A Tale of Two Siblings: Ella and Max's Lemonade Stand Venture

Ella and Max, a dynamic sister-brother duo at ages 10 and 12, decided to invest their lemonade stand earnings in stocks. They chose companies they knew and loved, like the makers of their favorite video games and snacks. It wasn't all smooth sailing. One of their chosen companies faced a recall, causing their shares to dip. But they held on, learning early that the market has good and bad days. Over time, their patience paid off, teaching them the critical lesson of sticking through the rough patches for eventual gain.

- **Lesson learned**: Even when the market looks grim, perseverance can lead to sweet rewards.
- **Advice**: "Invest in what you know and love. It makes the ups and downs more relatable," says Ella.

From Piggy Bank to Portfolio: Sarah's Journey

At 8, Sarah was given a few shares of a tech giant as a gift. Intrigued by the idea of owning a piece of a big company, she started doing chores and saving birthday money to buy more shares. By 14, Sarah had diversified her portfolio to include renewable energy and health-care stocks. She faced challenges, like when one stock plummeted due to an unexpected scandal. However, Sarah's diversified approach meant her overall portfolio remained strong.

- **Lesson learned**: Diversification is like a safety net, keeping you steady when individual investments fall.
- **Advice**: "Don't put all your eggs in one basket. Spread them out," Sarah advises.

The Accidental Investor: Liam's Story

Liam stumbled into investing at age 9 when he mistakenly clicked on an app advertisement offering virtual stock trading. With his parents' guidance, he began exploring the world of simulated stock investments, using virtual money to buy and sell. This safe, risk-free environment was the perfect playground for Liam to learn the ins and outs of the stock market, teaching him valuable lessons about research, timing, and market trends without any real-world losses.

- **Lesson learned**: Starting with simulated investments can be a fantastic, risk-free way to learn.
- **Advice**: "Use virtual trading apps to practice. It's like a video game, but you learn to invest," Liam suggests.

Starting Small, Dreaming Big: The Collective Wisdom

These stories underline a powerful message: Beginning your investing journey doesn't require a fortune. With just a few dollars and a dash of curiosity, any kid can embark on the path to becoming an investor. The key is to start small, stay patient, and keep learning. Here's a roundup of advice from our young investors:

- **Understand what you're investing in**: Take the time to learn about the companies or products you want to invest in.
- **Patience pays off**: Don't expect overnight success. Investing is about playing the long game.

- **Embrace mistakes**: Every misstep is a learning opportunity. Reflect on what went wrong and how you can improve.
- **Keep it fun**: Choose investments in businesses or sectors you're genuinely interested in. It makes the process enjoyable and personal.
- **Seek advice**: Don't be shy about asking parents, teachers, or financial advisors for insights. A little guidance can go a long way.

By weaving together these threads of wisdom, it becomes clear that investing isn't just for adults with big bank accounts. It's a realm where curious kids, armed with a bit of know-how and a lot of determination, can thrive and grow their financial futures.

As we wrap up this chapter, remember that the world of investing is vast and varied, offering endless opportunities to those willing to explore. From the stories of Ella, Max, Sarah, and Liam, we gather not just inspiration but also practical strategies for embarking on our own investing adventures. Whether it's through direct stock purchases, simulated trading apps, or starting with a simple savings account, the journey to financial growth begins with a single step. As we look ahead, let's carry forward the lessons learned, the advice shared, and the undeniable truth that age is just a number in the world of investing. The next chapter awaits, promising new financial landscapes to navigate and conquer.

CHAPTER 5
THE CREDIT CHRONICLE: NAVIGATING THE WORLD OF BORROWING WISELY

I magine you're at your favorite arcade. You've played all the games you're good at, racking up points like a pro. Now, you're eyeing the grand prize in the display case, but your points fall short. Here's where credit comes into play at the arcade of life. Instead of points, you're dealing with real money. Credit can be that bridge to reach what you want sooner, whether it's a new bike, a college education, or your first car. But, just like any arcade game, there are rules to play by to win.

5.1 THE BASICS OF BORROWING: GOOD DEBT VS. BAD DEBT

Credit is essentially a trust system. It's a way to borrow money with the promise to pay it back later, often with interest. Think of it like a friend lending you money to buy a game today because you don't have enough cash on hand, and you agree to pay them back after your next allowance. In this case, the friend is a bank or credit institution, and they'll charge you for the service.

Good Debt vs. Bad Debt

Not all debts are created equal. Some can actually work in your favor.

- **Good debt**: This is the kind that can help you advance in life. For example, taking a loan for college is seen as good debt. It's an investment in your education, potentially leading to better job opportunities and income in the future. Another example could be a mortgage for a house, which typically increases in value over time.
- **Bad debt**: This type usually results from buying things that won't increase in value and that you can't afford. High-interest credit card debt from buying the latest gadgets or designer clothes falls into this category. These items don't earn you money over time and might even lose value the moment you purchase them.

The Cost of Credit

Borrowing money isn't free. The extra cost comes in the form of interest, which can add up quicker than you'd expect. The interest rate, often a percentage, is what lenders charge you for borrowing money. It's like paying rent on the money you borrow.

- For example, if you take out a $100 loan with a 10% annual interest rate, you'll owe $110 at the end of the year. If you don't pay a loan off quickly, interest can make the total amount you owe grow larger and larger.

Building a Positive Credit History

Starting early on, building a good credit history can open doors for you in the future. Here's how to set yourself up for credit success:

- **Always pay on time**: This is the golden rule. Late payments can hurt your credit score, making it harder and more expensive to borrow money in the future.
- **Start small**: A low-limit credit card or a small loan, paid off regularly, can help you begin to build a good credit history.
- **Stay below your limit**: Try not to max out your credit cards. Using a small portion of your available credit looks better on your credit report.
- **Monitor your credit**: Know your credit score and look at your credit report. This way, you can catch any mistakes and understand how your behavior with money affects your credit.

Debt Responsibility Quiz

Take this quiz to see how well you understand the concepts of good and bad debt, interest rates, and the basics of credit. Each question gives feedback and tips to improve your borrowing smarts.

1. What is debt?

A. Money that you find on the street.
B. Money that you earn from a job.
C. Money that you borrow from someone else and need to pay back.
D. Money that you keep in a piggy bank.

Answer: Debt is money that you borrow from someone else, like a bank or a friend, which you need to pay back later, often with extra money called interest. (Answer C)

Feedback & tips: Remember, borrowing should be done wisely. Always ask yourself if what you're borrowing for is necessary or if it can wait until you have enough money saved up.

2. Can debt be a good thing?

A. No, because it's always bad to owe money.
B. Yes, when you use it to buy all the video games you want.
C. Yes, when it's used for something that benefits you in the long run.
D. No, because you should never spend money.

Answer: Yes, debt can be good when it's used for something that will benefit you in the long run, like an education that helps you get a better job. (Answer C)

Feedback & tips: Think of good debt as an investment in your future. But be careful to only borrow what you need and can pay back comfortably.

3. What is bad debt?

A. Borrowing money to buy a house.
B. Money borrowed for things that lose value quickly.
C. Taking a loan for education.
D. Saving money in a bank.

Answer: Bad debt is money borrowed for things that lose value quickly or don't provide a return on your investment, like spending on toys or a fancy vacation. (Answer B)

Feedback & tips: Before making a purchase with borrowed money, consider if it's something you really need or if there's a cheaper alternative.

4. What are interest rates?

A. A fee you pay to use a shopping cart.
B. The extra percentage of borrowed money you pay to the lender.
C. The rate at which your pocket money increases.
D. A type of rate used in cooking recipes.

Answer: Interest rates are the percentage of the borrowed amount you have to pay extra to the lender for allowing you to use their money. (Answer B)

Feedback & tips: Always look for the lowest interest rate when borrowing money. You'll always have to pay more than you borrowed, but higher rates mean you'll have to pay even more extra.

5. How does credit work?

    A. By only using cash for purchases.
    B. It allows you to borrow money or buy things with a
       promise to pay back later.
    C. It works like magic.
    D. You get unlimited money.

Answer: Credit allows you to borrow money to buy things with a promise to pay the money back later. Good credit means you're trusted to pay back the money on time. (Answer B)

Feedback & tips: Always pay back borrowed money on time to build good credit. This shows lenders that you're responsible with money.

6. What happens if you don't pay back debt?

    A. You may face extra fees, higher interest rates, and a lower
       credit score.
    B. You get a reward.
    C. Nothing happens.
    D. You receive more money.

Answer: Not paying back debt can lead to extra fees, higher interest rates, and a lower credit score. This means it will be harder to borrow money in the future. (Answer A)

Feedback & tips: If you're having trouble paying back debt, talk to the lender right away to discuss your options. They may be able to help you with a payment plan.

7. Why is budgeting important when you have debt?

    A. Because it's a fun hobby.
    B. It helps you manage your spending to ensure you can pay
       back your debts.
    C. Budgeting is not important.
    D. It increases your debt.

Answer: Budgeting helps you keep track of your spending and make sure you have enough money to pay back your debts while still covering your other expenses. (Answer B)

Feedback & tips: Start a simple budget by listing your income and expenses. This will help you see where your money is going and find ways to save.

8. What is a savings account, and how can it help with debt?

    A. A type of game.
    B. A book where you write down your debts.
    C. A tool to create more debt.
    D. A place to keep your money that earns interest and can
       help avoid debt.

Answer: A savings account is a place to keep your money that earns interest over time. Having savings can help you avoid debt by giving you a cushion for unexpected expenses. (Answer D)

Feedback & tips: Try to save a small portion of your allowance or gift money regularly. Over time, this can grow and help you pay for big purchases without going into debt.

9. How can you avoid bad debt?

A. By spending all your money quickly.
B. By thinking carefully before borrowing and planning how to pay it back.
C. By borrowing as much money as possible.
D. By hiding your money.

Answer: You can avoid bad debt by thinking carefully before borrowing money, considering if you really need what you're borrowing for, and planning how you'll pay it back. (Answer B)

Feedback & tips: Always ask yourself, "Is this something I need or just want?" If it's just a want, it's better to save up for it instead of going into debt.

10. What should you do before taking on any debt?

A. Tell all your friends.
B. Research and understand the terms, and make sure you can afford to pay it back.
C. Spend all your current money.
D. Take a nap.

Answer: Before taking on any debt, research and understand the terms, like the interest rate and the payment schedule. Make sure you have the ability to pay it back on time. (Answer B)

Feedback & tips: Talking to a trusted adult about your plan to borrow money can give you a new perspective and help you make a smart decision about taking on debt.

Checklist for Healthy Credit Habits

- Pay bills on time, every time.
- Keep credit card balances well below your credit limits.
- Only apply for credit when absolutely necessary.
- Regularly check your credit report for accuracy (Have an adult help you with this.).
- Educate yourself on financial terms and rights as a borrower.

Building a positive relationship with credit doesn't have to be daunting. By understanding the basics of borrowing, distinguishing between good and bad debt, and adopting healthy credit habits early on, you can navigate the credit world like a pro. Remember, when used wisely, credit can be a powerful tool in achieving your financial goals.

5.2 THE DANGERS OF DEBT: WHY TO BE CAREFUL

Navigating the world of credit is like playing a game where the rules keep changing. It's exciting and can be rewarding, but there are pitfalls that can easily trip you up if you're not paying close attention. Understanding these pitfalls is crucial to playing the game smartly and keeping yourself on the path to financial well-being. Even if you're not currently borrowing money, understanding these dangers early on is important. By the time you're ready to venture out on your own, you'll have a head start, easily navigating past the money missteps that could trap your peers.

Compounding Interest on Debt

First, let's talk about how compounding interest can turn a small debt into a mountain. Unlike the interest in a savings account that works in your favor, interest on debt can quickly become your adversary. Imagine you owe money on a credit card. Each month, interest is added to your outstanding balance. The next month, you owe interest on the new balance, which now includes the previous month's interest. If you only make minimum payments, this cycle can make the amount you owe grow out of control.

Look at it this way, if your debt is a snowball rolling down a hill, compounding interest is the snow on the ground, making that ball bigger and bigger as it rolls.

Credit Card Traps

Credit cards, while useful, are loaded with traps for the unwary. The convenience and rewards they offer can be enticing, but they come with strings attached. It's never too early to learn about how they work.

- **Minimum payments**: Paying only the minimum payment due each month might seem like a relief for your wallet, but it's a slow drain on your financial health. This practice stretches your debt over years, inflating the total amount you pay because of compound interest.
- **High interest rates**: Credit cards most often have higher interest rates than other forms of debt. This rate can spike even higher if you miss a payment or your account is not in good standing.
- **Fees and penalties**: Late fees, annual fees, and charges for

exceeding your credit limit can add up, eating into your budget.

Managing Existing Debt

Hopefully, you will avoid the stress of getting into debt while you're young because facing a pile of debt can feel like confronting a dragon in its den. With a strategic approach, however, you can tame the beast if you ever find yourself in this situation.

Here are some strategies:

- **Snowball method**: Focus on paying off your smallest debts first while making minimum payments on others. Once the smallest debt is cleared, move to the next smallest, and so on. This method can create momentum and a sense of achievement.
- **Avalanche method**: Alternatively, tackle debts with the highest interest rates first, regardless of the balance. This approach can save you money in the long run by reducing the amount of interest you'll pay.
- **Negotiating terms**: Reach out to your creditors to discuss more favorable repayment terms. You might be surprised at their willingness to work with you during tough times.

The Impact of Debt on Financial Goals

Debt doesn't just affect your current finances. It can also put future dreams on hold. Whether it's buying a home, traveling, or starting a business, debt can divert funds that would otherwise go toward these goals. It's like trying to fill a bucket with water when there's a hole in the bottom. No matter how much you pour in, you never seem to make progress.

- Think of your financial goals as the places you want to go on a map. Debt is the detour that takes you off your planned route, making it harder for you to get started on your journey.

Remember, debt isn't inherently bad. When used wisely, it's a tool that can help you achieve your goals. However, it demands respect and understanding. By recognizing the dangers of debt, you can confidently navigate the credit landscape, keeping your financial future bright and within reach.

5.3 CREDIT CARDS FOR KIDS: WHAT YOU NEED TO KNOW

Navigating the world of spending doesn't just involve knowing how much money you have in your piggy bank or savings account. In today's swipe-and-go society, understanding the difference between debit and credit cards is like learning to read a new language, one that can significantly impact your financial health if not understood properly.

Debit vs. Credit

So you've probably seen adults swiping or tapping their cards at stores without exchanging any cash. Most times, they're using one of two types of cards: debit or credit. Here's how they stack up against each other:

- Debit cards are direct lines to your bank account. Think of them as digital keys that unlock your own money vault. The cost is deducted from your account right away when you buy something. It's like having an invisible wallet that holds exactly what you have—no more, no less.
- Credit cards, however, are more like taking a loan for every purchase you make. The bank pays the store for you, and you agree to pay the bank back. The catch here is that you're not spending your money. You're spending the bank's money, and they'll charge you interest if you don't pay it back in time.

Getting the hang of using a debit card can be a great first step into the world of financial independence. It helps you practice spending only what you have, which is a golden rule for healthy finances.

Prepaid Credit Cards for Practice

Before diving into the ocean of credit, dipping your toes into a shallower pool might be wise. Enter prepaid credit cards. These are fantastic tools for learning the ropes of credit card management without the risk of sinking into debt. Here's why:

- You load prepaid cards with a set amount of money. Once it's gone, it's gone. You can't spend any more until you reload the card.
- Prepaid cards mimic the experience of using a credit card, including online purchases, without the danger of spending beyond your means.
- They're great for practicing budgeting. You can only spend what's on the card, making it easier to track and control your spending.

Understanding Credit Card Terms

Credit card agreements might seem like they're written in an ancient, mystical language. Here's a quick decoder for some of the terms you'll come across:

- APR (Annual Percentage Rate) shows the interest rate for a whole year, not just a month. It's how much the bank will charge you for borrowing their money.
- Your credit limit is the highest amount you can borrow on the card. Going over this limit usually results in extra fees.
- Late fees are what you pay if you miss the deadline for your monthly payment. These can add up and hurt your credit score, so always aim to pay on time.

By understanding these terms, you're better equipped to choose and use a credit card wisely, ensuring it becomes a tool for building your financial future, not a trap.

Safe Credit Practices

Keeping a few safety tips in mind can turn a credit card from a potential headache into a handy financial tool:

- Only use it for purchases you can afford. If you can't buy something with the cash you have now, think twice before charging it to your credit card.
- Always aim to pay off the full balance each month. This way, you avoid paying interest and you keep your credit score healthy.
- Keep track of your spending. Regularly check your account online to ensure you're not nearing your credit limit and to spot any suspicious activity.

- Know when to say no. Just because you have a credit limit doesn't mean you need to use it. Treat your credit card use with the same caution and consideration as spending physical cash.

Navigating credit successfully comes down to understanding the tools at your disposal, setting clear boundaries for yourself, and always aiming for practices that boost, rather than bust, your financial health. With these principles in hand, even the youngest spenders can start to build a credit history that opens doors to a healthy financial future.

5.4 BUILDING GOOD CREDIT: STARTING EARLY

Having a solid credit score is like holding a key that can unlock numerous doors in your future. It allows you to borrow money for big purchases later on, smooths the way to snagging that apartment you've been eyeing, and even sways potential employers who might check your credit as part of their hiring process. Let's explore some smart moves you can make to start building a strong credit foundation early on.

Co-Signed Accounts: A Team Effort

Getting into the credit game can be tricky without a history to show you're a safe bet. This is where having a co-signed account comes into play. It's like teaming up with someone who's already established good credit, such as a parent or guardian, to open an account. Their credit reputation gives lenders the confidence to take a chance on you. Using this account responsibly—think timely payments and smart spending—starts building your credit history. It's a partnership, so remember, any missteps not only affect your credit but also your co-signer's. Communication and responsibility are key.

Reporting Rent and Utility Payments: Everyday Credits

You might not know this, but the regular payments you make in the future for rent or utilities can also help build your credit history. Normally, these payments don't automatically show up on your credit report. However, services are available that can report these payments for you, turning your monthly rent and utility bills into opportunities to boost your credit score. It's like getting extra credit for homework you're already doing! Just make sure you're consistently making these payments on time because, like with any credit activity, late payments can ding your score.

Monitoring Credit: Keeping an Eye on Your Financial Pulse

As you get older and start building credit, staying informed about your credit status is crucial. Regularly checking your credit report keeps you up to date with your score and helps you make sure the information is accurate. Mistakes happen, and they can drag down your credit score if not corrected. Think of checking your credit report as doing a health check-up on your finances. You want to catch any errors early, from misreported late payments to accounts you don't recognize, which could be signs of identity theft. Most importantly, understanding the factors that influence your credit score gives you insights into how to improve it over time.

- Start by checking your credit report annually. It's free and doesn't affect your score.
- If you spot errors, report them immediately to the credit bureau for correction.

- Watching your credit score improve can be motivating, showing you the direct impact of your financial habits.

Building good credit is like a marathon, not a sprint. It requires patience, consistency, and smart habits. Remember, your credit score reflects your financial habits over time. By being responsible with a co-signed account, ensuring your regular payments are counted toward your credit history, and keeping a close watch on your credit report, you're laying a strong foundation for your financial future. These steps might seem small, but they're mighty in their ability to shape your credit journey positively.

As we wrap up this chapter, think of building good credit as planting a garden. It takes time, care, and a bit of daily attention, but the rewards—access to loans, better interest rates, and more financial opportunities—are well worth the effort. Keep nurturing your financial garden, and you'll be amazed at how it grows. Now, let's turn the page and discover more strategies for financial success.

YOUR REVIEW CAN SPARK A FINANCIAL REVOLUTION

Be the Hero in Someone's Financial Journey

"Every penny saved is a step towards a brighter future."

A TWIST ON BENJAMIN FRANKLIN.

Hey there, amazing young minds and the guardians of our future! Have you ever imagined turning your pocket money into a treasure chest, or better yet, becoming a financial superhero for someone just like you? Well, buckle up, because that's exactly the kind of adventure we're on with "The Ultimate Guide to Financial Literacy for Kids" by Money Mentor Publications.

Now, I've got a super important mission for you, should you choose to accept it.

Would you believe me if I told you that you could light up someone else's path to financial wisdom with just a few taps and a sprinkle of your thoughts? It's true! Like you, countless young adventurers are out there, eager to learn the secrets of saving, spending wisely, and growing their money trees. But here's the thing - they might not know where to start or which guide to trust on this thrilling journey.

This is where your superpowers come into play. Believe it or not, your words have the power to launch a thousand ships... or in this case, kickstart a thousand financial journeys!

Here's my heart-to-heart ask, from one bright spark to another:

Please take a moment to share your thoughts and leave this book a review.

Think of it as dropping a message in a bottle into the vast ocean of the internet. Your review could be the beacon that guides another young navigator to safe financial shores. And guess what? It won't cost you a dime, just a minute of your time, but the impact could be priceless.

Here's how you can unleash your superpower:

1. Grab your gadget and scan the QR code below.
2. Share your journey with "The Ultimate Guide to Financial Literacy for Kids".

https://www.amazon.com/review/create-review/?asin= B0CZDGZGFG

If the thought of helping someone find their way makes your heart do a happy dance, then you, my friend, are a true hero. Welcome to the league of extraordinary financial wizards!

Thank you from every corner of my heart (and wallet). Now, let's dive back into our treasure trove of tips and tricks.

- Your biggest cheerleader, Money Mentor Publications

CHAPTER 6

DIGITAL DOLLARS AND SENSE: NAVIGATING FINANCE IN THE TECH AGE

Think of a world where your piggy bank gets smarter every day, learning the best ways to guard and grow your money. Now imagine this piggy bank isn't made of porcelain or plastic but bytes and pixels living inside your smartphone or tablet. Welcome to the modern era of managing money, where technology is not just an add-on to your financial journey, it's the vehicle driving you forward. In this chapter, we dive into the digital tools that make handling money easier and more fun.

First, let's tackle some tools revolutionizing how kids (and adults) think about and manage their finances: budgeting apps.

6.1 BUDGETING APPS FOR KIDS: TECH-SAVVY SAVING

The Role of Technology in Finance

When your parents were young, they kept track of their money by jotting down notes in a diary or trying to memorize what they spent at the candy store. Those days are fading fast, thanks to technology. Now apps can do the heavy lifting, tracking every dollar earned from mowing lawns or every penny saved for that new video game. They can even categorize your spending automatically, showing you where your money goes in colorful charts and graphs. It's like having a financial advisor in your pocket, one that's fun and friendly.

Top Budgeting Apps for Kids

- **Allowance & Chores Bot**: Imagine an app that helps you manage your chores and allowance all in one place. This app tracks the tasks you've completed and shows your earnings and spending. It's like a digital ledger that's easy to follow, which makes it perfect for keeping an eye on your financial goals.
- **GoHenry**: With features designed to teach money management through real-life experience, this app comes with a debit card just for kids. Parents control where and how the card can be used, making it a safe way to practice spending and saving in the digital world.
- **Bankaroo**: Created by a kid for kids, this app is all about making finance fun. It uses virtual money to help track savings goals, spending, and even charitable giving. It's a great first step into the world of budgeting without having to use real money.

Privacy and Security

With great power comes great responsibility, especially when that power is in an app. Using financial apps means sharing some personal information, which is why it's critical to understand privacy and security. Always:

- Ask a parent to help you check the app's privacy policy to see how your information is used and protected.
- Use strong passwords and never share them.
- Regularly review transactions and talk to a parent if anything looks off.

Remember, keeping your digital dollars safe is as important as protecting cash in a wallet.

Engaging With Parents

Don't fly solo on your financial voyage. These apps are an excellent way for you and your parents to talk about money matters together. Discussing savings goals, spending limits, and even charitable giving can turn into a family affair, making money management a shared adventure.

- Schedule regular check-ins to go over the app together. Discuss what you've learned and any adjustments you might want to make to your budget or savings goals.
- Use the app as a conversation starter for bigger financial discussions, like saving for college or understanding credit.

Technology has transformed the way we interact with money, making it more accessible, understandable, and engaging than ever before. With the right tools and a bit of curiosity, diving into the world of finance becomes an adventure, not a chore. As we continue to explore the digital world of money management, remember that these tools are here to serve you, helping to sculpt a financial future that's bright, informed, and full of potential.

6.2 CREATING A FINANCIAL JOURNAL: TRACKING YOUR MONEY

Imagine having a magic book that remembers where every cent of your allowance went and shows you how to make smarter money moves in the future. This is what happens when you start keeping a financial journal. It's your personal finance story, written by you, filled with insights into your spending habits and progress toward your goals.

Benefits of Journaling

A financial journal acts as your money mirror, reflecting back on your spending behaviors, saving patterns, and the journey toward your financial goals. It can highlight habits you didn't know you had, like that sneaky tendency to splurge on snacks after school. From putting pen to paper or tapping those keys, you start to see patterns, both good and bad. This awareness is the first step toward making change. Plus, recording your victories, no matter how small, can boost your motivation to keep going.

- **Insight**: Discover patterns in your spending and savings that you might not see otherwise.
- **Accountability**: Writing down your goals and keeping track of your progress keeps you accountable.
- **Motivation**: Celebrating your successes, big and small, keeps the motivation fire burning.

What to Track

Your financial journal can be as unique as you are, but there are a few key elements worth keeping tabs on:

- **Income**: This could be your allowance, money from odd jobs, or birthday cash. Knowing what money is coming in is crucial.
- **Expenses**: Track where your money's going, from the necessary (school supplies) to the fun (movies with friends).
- **Savings**: Keep a record of what you're saving for and how much you've tucked away. Watching this number grow can be super satisfying.
- **Financial goals**: Write down your goals, both short-term (a new game, for instance) and long-term (saving for a car). Seeing them in black and white makes them feel more achievable.

Journaling Methods

The beauty of a financial journal is that it can be anything you want it to be. Here are a couple of ways to get started:

- **Pen and paper**: There's something special about writing things down the old-fashioned way. A dedicated notebook where you write down your financial observations can be a tangible reminder of your money journey. Plus, you can get creative with colored pens and stickers to make it your own.
- **Digital journaling**: If you're more tech-inclined, numerous apps and software can serve as your digital journal. They offer the convenience of having your financial info at your fingertips, often with added features like automatic categorization and visual charts. Work with a parent to choose the one that would work best for you, and make sure to back up your data to avoid losing your valuable insights.

Review and Reflect

The real power of a financial journal lies in regularly sitting down to review and reflect on what you've written. This helps you recognize where you can improve and acknowledge what you're doing right. Set aside a time each week to go through your journal. Ask yourself:

- What was my biggest financial win this week?
- Did I make any impulse purchases? What led to them?
- How am I progressing toward my financial goals?
- What can I do differently next week to improve?

This practice lets you keep track of numbers and understand the why behind your financial decisions. It turns your journal into a tool for growth, helping you make smarter choices in the future.

Keeping a financial journal is like drawing your own map in the treasure hunt of personal finance. It guides you through the forests of spending, over the mountains of saving, and toward the goals you've set for yourself. With every entry, you're writing the story of your financial journey, one page at a time.

6.3 ONLINE BANKING BASICS FOR THE YOUNG SAVER

Gone are the days when saving meant stuffing crumpled notes and jingling coins into an old, dusty piggy bank. The banking world has taken a giant leap into the digital realm, making managing your money just a click or tap away. But what exactly is online banking, and how does it work? Think of it as your digital wallet, always ready, always accessible, wherever you have access to a phone or tablet.

Online Banking Simplified

Online banking lets you handle your money without visiting a physical bank. Imagine being able to check how much money you have, move some of it to a friend as a birthday gift, or save a chunk of it for that dream hoverboard—all from your device. It's banking at your fingertips, on your schedule and not the bank's.

Features of Online Banking

Diving a bit deeper, online banking comes with a lot of features designed to make your life easier. Here are a few you might find super handy:

- **Checking your balance**: Know exactly how much money you have at any moment. It's like having a financial mirror that reflects your current money situation, helping you make informed spending decisions.
- **Money transfers**: Want to split the cost of a gift or pay back a friend? Online banking lets you transfer money in a snap, often without any fees, especially if the recipient is with the same bank.
- **Mobile deposits**: Did you receive a check for your birthday? No need to run to the bank. Just take a picture with your phone and deposit it through your banking app. Magic? Almost.
- **Bill payments**: Though more relevant for adults, it's cool to know that bills can be paid directly through online banking.

Safety Tips for Online Banking

As always, having all this power comes with responsibility, especially when it comes to keeping your digital dollars safe. Here are some golden rules for secure online banking:

- **Strong passwords**: Your first line of defense. Mix letters, numbers, and special characters to create a password that's tough to crack.
- **Phishing scam awareness**: Scammers might try to trick you into giving them your banking info. Your bank will *never* ask for your password or PIN via email or text. If someone is asking, they're trying to trick you.
- **Public Wi-Fi caution**: Using public Wi-Fi for banking is like leaving your wallet open on a park bench. If you need to bank on the go, use your data plan or a secure VPN.
- **Log out after every session**: Just like you wouldn't leave your house door open when you leave, always log out of your banking app when you're done.

The Future of Banking

Peering into the crystal ball of banking, we see a world where cryptocurrencies and blockchain technology play bigger roles.

- Cryptocurrencies are like special online coins that are kept safe with secret codes. They don't belong to any bank or country. You might know names like Bitcoin or Ethereum. These special coins could change the way we use and think about our allowance or savings in the future.
- Blockchain technology is the backbone of cryptocurrencies. It's a system of recording information in a way that makes it

difficult or impossible to change or cheat. It could make banking even more secure and transparent in the future.

Online banking is more than just a convenience, it's a shift in how we interact with money, blending security with accessibility. As banking continues evolving with advancements like cryptocurrencies and blockchain, staying informed and cautious ensures your digital financial journey is exciting and safe. Let's take a deeper dive, shall we?

6.4 THE FUTURE OF MONEY: DIGITAL CURRENCIES AND KIDS

Imagine a world where money isn't something you hold in your hand. Instead, it's a digital code on your computer or phone. This isn't out of a sci-fi movie, it's the reality of digital currencies, also known as cryptocurrencies. Unlike the dollars or coins in your pocket, digital currencies aren't printed or minted by governments. They exist entirely online and are created and held electronically.

Breaking Down Digital Currencies

At their core, digital currencies are a form of money that's available only in digital or electronic form. Bitcoin, the first and most well-known cryptocurrency, popped onto the scene in 2009, opening the floodgates to a whole new way of thinking about money. Cryptocurrencies use blockchain, which is like a big online notebook that keeps track of everyone's digital coin trades without needing a bank. It's like if you traded stickers directly with your friends without anyone else needing to check or approve the trade. This makes it a system where people can exchange digital coins directly with each other.

Using Digital Money

You might wonder how digital currencies fit into your life as a kid. While you're not likely to invest in Bitcoin anytime soon, you're already encountering digital money in different forms:

- **Online gaming currencies**: Many online games have their own form of currency, like Robux in Roblox or V-Bucks in Fortnite. These virtual currencies are used to buy in-game items or upgrades and are a simple, kid-friendly introduction to digital money.
- **Gift cards**: Have you ever received a digital gift card? It's another form of digital currency. You use a code to redeem the card online, exchanging it for goods or services without touching physical money.

Risks and Considerations

While digital currencies offer exciting possibilities, they come with their own set of challenges:

- **Volatility**: Volatility means something can change quickly and unpredictably. That means the value of cryptocurrencies can vary greatly from one day to the next. This unpredictability makes them a risky investment because their worth can significantly increase or decrease quickly.
- **Understanding value**: Grasping the concept of digital money's value can be tricky since it's not something you can physically see or touch. It's important to learn how to equate digital currencies with real-world money to understand what you're spending or potentially earning.

Financial Literacy in a Digital Age

As the world becomes more digital, financial literacy means you need to know about more than counting cash or saving in a bank. You have to navigate the digital financial landscape. Understanding digital currencies and how they operate is becoming an essential skill. You need to know how to do it and be aware of the risks, the security measures needed to protect digital assets, and the ethical considerations of using such technologies.

- **Embrace curiosity**: Dive into learning about digital currencies and blockchain technology. The more you know, the better prepared you'll be for the financial world of tomorrow.
- **Stay cautious**: While exploring digital money, always remember the importance of security. Protecting your digital wallet is as crucial as safeguarding physical money.
- **Think ahead**: As you save and plan for the future, consider how digital currencies might play a role in your financial strategies. The landscape of money and investment is evolving, and staying informed will keep you ahead of the curve.

In wrapping up this glimpse into the future of money, it's clear that the financial world kids are growing into is very different from previous generations. Digital currencies, with their blend of technology and finance, are paving new roads for transactions, savings, and investments. Understanding these digital assets, their benefits, and their risks is crucial for anyone looking to successfully navigate tomorrow's financial waters. As we move forward, keep an open mind, stay informed, and approach the digital financial realm with both enthusiasm and caution. This balance will serve you well as you step into the future of money equipped with the knowledge and skills to thrive in an increasingly digital world. Now, let's turn the page, ready to tackle new adventures in personal finance.

Chapter 6 Review Activity

```
R  S  N  B  T  Z  X  B  J  N  S  G  T  C  D  Y  C  T  C  W  Z  X
W  K  O  D  J  L  Y  R  S  O  T  Q  P  R  E  D  K  Q  Y  O  G  I
G  R  L  C  X  A  P  F  A  P  P  S  Z  Y  A  U  R  T  J  Y  G  B
P  L  Y  F  T  U  U  D  A  U  N  X  H  P  Y  N  I  P  C  G  E  L
K  M  V  Q  I  S  E  Y  P  C  U  C  P  T  Q  R  S  V  Z  P  X  O
R  P  P  V  N  N  W  Q  A  G  V  E  G  O  U  D  B  F  V  K  G  C
B  D  I  G  I  T  A  L  D  E  X  N  P  C  P  X  Q  J  E  D  P  K
F  I  N  A  N  C  E  N  Y  F  I  D  E  U  Q  C  J  G  U  R  A  C
C  U  T  G  U  X  B  L  C  K  D  S  H  R  Y  Z  P  E  D  S  S  H
W  B  U  C  W  F  N  R  N  I  C  N  M  R  Y  R  U  B  S  Q  S  A
N  T  H  G  O  Q  J  A  V  Z  A  E  R  E  V  E  E  O  E  P  W  I
R  F  D  Q  N  I  B  H  S  F  L  L  T  N  I  R  B  M  O  N  O  N
C  Q  Z  I  I  E  N  U  A  C  P  N  L  C  B  R  S  X  E  Q  R  A
U  K  R  R  N  W  U  T  V  A  M  H  Y  I  C  N  Y  L  I  D  D  S
Y  U  L  I  G  E  Y  A  I  D  M  J  I  E  T  K  X  Y  I  A  S  Y
A  N  L  O  N  I  J  N  N  U  S  L  Z  S  I  E  F  N  K  N  N  C
N  N  U  R  H  D  G  S  G  V  L  K  N  Q  H  F  R  O  E  G  E  C
O  U  M  H  M  U  F  I  S  I  H  D  Y  Z  D  I  K  A  M  Q  W  C
Y  P  E  T  M  D  G  A  G  O  H  E  N  R  Y  Y  N  O  C  I  D  S
I  P  V  B  X  A  M  V  Z  Q  G  E  E  F  C  R  J  G  I  Y  X  I
Q  G  D  Y  K  T  Z  J  W  R  Q  R  T  S  X  V  I  A  M  D  C  T
V  C  L  F  D  E  C  X  Y  Y  Q  P  W  W  C  Y  W  I  U  V  R  Q
```

Digital	Finance	Apps
Savings	GoHenry	Security
Cryptocurrencies	Blockchain	Online Banking
Transfers	Passwords	Bitcoin
Financial Literacy	Phishing	

Answer Key on Page 162

CHAPTER 7
NAVIGATING MONEY MISSTEPS

I magine waking up one morning to find that your favorite game, which used to cost 10 coins, now costs 20 coins. Frustrating, right? It's a bit like life. Sometimes, things don't go as planned, especially when it comes to managing our money. This chapter is your map for dodging financial pitfalls and making smarter moves with your money. Money missteps are like tripping over a rake in the yard. They're bound to happen, but with some care, you can avoid a cartoonish faceplant.

7.1 COMMON MONEY BLUNDERS KIDS MAKE

Overspending on Trends

It's hard not to want the latest sneakers or the newest phone everyone's talking about. But constantly chasing trends can lead to spending more money than you have. Remember, trends come and go. Today's must-have item can quickly become tomorrow's garage sale bargain. So, before you spend, ask yourself, "Will I still use this a month from now?" If the answer is "probably not," you might want to rethink that purchase.

Neglecting to Save

Sometimes, saving money feels like a chore, especially when there's something shiny and new catching your eye. But not stashing away part of your allowance or birthday money can leave you high and dry when you really need or want something. Start small, even a little bit saved regularly can add up over time. Think of saving as paying your future self. It's like planting a seed that eventually grows into a money tree you can harvest later.

Giving In to Peer Pressure

We've all been there. Your friend shows off a new gadget, and suddenly, you feel like you need one, too, even if it means spending all your savings. Peer pressure is tough, but remember, true friends won't judge you based on what you have or don't have. It's okay to say no or suggest a more budget-friendly activity. Your wallet will thank you.

Here's a toolkit of responses that can help you stand your ground when faced with peer pressure, especially regarding spending money. Try these ready-to-use scripts:

When Friends Want You to Buy Expensive Things

- Response: "I'm saving up for something special, so I can't join in on buying that right now."

When Everyone is Getting the Latest Gadget

- Response: "It looks cool, but my old one still works fine. I'd rather save my money for something else."

When Being Teased for Not Having Brand-Name Items

- Response: "Brands don't really matter to me. I like what I have, and that's enough."

When Encouraged to Spend All Your Money at Once

- Response: "I'm learning to manage my money better. Part of that is not spending it all in one place."

When Invited to Expensive Outings

- Response: "That sounds fun, but it's a bit too pricey for me. Can we do something less expensive instead?"

When Pressured to Lend Money

- Response: "I'm really careful about where my money goes. I can't lend it out, but I'm here to help you figure out another solution."

When Everyone Wants to Pool Money for a Big Purchase

- Response: "I'm on a tight budget and have to pass this time. Maybe next time we can plan something that fits everyone's budget."

When Friends Mock You for Budgeting

- Response: "Budgeting helps me keep track of my money and spend it on things I really want or need. I think it's pretty smart."

When Being Called Cheap for Not Spending Freely

- Response: "I prefer to think of it as being smart with my money. Saving now means I can enjoy something even better later."

When Tempted to Buy Just to Fit In

- Response: "I'd rather save my money for things I'm truly excited about, not just to keep up with everyone else."

Practicing these scripts can help you feel more prepared and secure in your decisions when faced with financial peer pressure.

Forgetting About Future Needs

Thinking ahead isn't just for grown-ups. Whether it's saving for a new game that's coming out in six months or setting aside money for a school trip, planning for future expenses ensures you won't be caught off guard. It's like packing an umbrella on a cloudy day. You might not need it, but you'll be glad to have it if it rains.

- Reflection: What's one thing you wish you had saved for but didn't? How would saving for it have made a difference? As you write, think about the impact of saving on achieving your goals.

Navigating money missteps isn't going to be perfect, but you'll learn, adjust, and make smarter decisions next time. Whether you've splurged on a fleeting trend, forgotten to feed your piggy bank, caved to the call of the crowd, or overlooked future needs, each mistake is a stepping stone to becoming more financially savvy. Remember, the best financial plan is the one that works for you, grows with you, and helps you dodge those metaphorical rakes in the yard of life.

7.2 LESSONS FROM MONEY MISTAKES: GROWING SMARTER

Mistakes, especially those involving money, often feel like stumbling blocks. Yet they're hidden gems packed with insights ready to be uncovered. This part of our adventure shines a light on the silver linings found in financial missteps, showcasing how they can sculpt us into more savvy money managers.

Learning From Experience

Diving into tales where kids faced financial oops moments can be enlightening. Picture Zack, who once spent his entire summer savings on a fancy remote-controlled car, only to find it gathering dust a week later. The initial thrill faded, leaving Zack with a valuable lesson: Instant gratification often leads to lasting regret. Or consider Maya, who, in a bid to keep up appearances, bought trendy sneakers that plunged her savings into the red—they cost more than she had saved. The experience taught her the importance of living within her means, setting her on a path to more mindful spending.

These narratives aren't just stories. They're windows into the consequences of our choices, teaching us to pause and ponder before making similar decisions.

The Role of Setbacks

Encountering a financial setback can feel like hitting a roadblock on your path to saving glory. Yet it's in these moments that growth sprouts. Each setback, be it an impulsive buy that empties your wallet or a forgotten savings goal, is a step toward better financial habits. Through these experiences, we learn resilience, discovering that bouncing back with a smarter plan is always possible. This resilience builds a financial backbone sturdy enough to support smarter decisions in the future.

Asking for Advice

When money matters get confusing, asking for help can make things a lot clearer. Sometimes, kids might be scared to ask questions because they don't want to be judged for making mistakes. But talking to parents, teachers, or someone else who knows a lot about money can help you see things you didn't notice before. These talks can make the tricky parts of dealing with money easier to understand. They're a chance to learn from others who have been through their own money adventures and can guide you on what to do.

- Have a family meeting about money every month. Talk about what you hope to do with your money, any problems you've had, and what you've done well.
- Talk in class about a money choice you made recently. Ask your friends and teacher what they think and if they have any other ideas on what you could do.
- If you can, meet with a money expert to make plans. They can help you figure out how to reach your money goals.

Adapting and Adjusting

The financial landscape is ever-changing, much like the seasons. A strategy that worked brilliantly last year might not fit this year's goals or challenges. This fluidity demands flexibility, the willingness to tweak and refine your financial plan to ensure it remains aligned with your evolving needs and aspirations. It's about staying dynamic, ready to adjust sails when the financial winds shift. This adaptability ensures that your money management strategies grow with you, always reflecting your current reality and future dreams.

- Regularly review your financial goals, asking if they still meet your aspirations.
- Experiment with different saving techniques or budgeting apps to find what works best for you.
- Reflect on past financial mistakes, considering how different strategies could prevent similar outcomes.

In essence, the journey through financial missteps to smarter money management is paved with lessons waiting to be learned. Each stumble, each fall, is a chance to rise stronger, equipped with newfound wisdom. Through these experiences, we become not just wise spenders and savers but also resilient navigators of our financial futures.

7.3 THE IMPORTANCE OF FINANCIAL DISCIPLINE

In the world of money matters, being disciplined is like having a superpower. It's the key to unlocking your goals, one saved coin at a time. But what does it really mean to be financially disciplined? Think of it as making decisions today that will make you proud tomorrow. It's about choosing to save instead of spend, and planning instead of splurging.

What is Financial Discipline?

Financial discipline is the practice of making decisions about your money that are in line with your long-term goals. It's not about never having fun or spending money; it's about knowing when and how to do so wisely. This might mean waiting a bit longer to buy that new game so you can keep your savings on track or choosing to do extra chores to earn more money before making a purchase. Essentially, it's learning how to control your impulses so they don't control you.

Building Self-Control

Gaining control over your spending and saving habits doesn't happen overnight. It's built through small, daily choices. Here are a few strategies to help you develop this important skill:

- **Pause before purchasing**: Give yourself a cooling-off period before buying something non-essential. Sometimes the urge to buy fades if you give it a little time.
- **Needs vs. wants list**: Keep a list of items you need versus things you want. Prioritize spending on your needs before your wants.
- **Visual reminders**: Place pictures of your savings goals around your room or set them as backgrounds on your devices. Seeing what you're saving for can help keep you focused.

Developing self-control is part practice, part patience. It's normal to slip up now and then. The key is to learn from those experiences and keep moving forward.

Setting and Sticking to Budgets

A budget is like a blueprint for your financial goals. It gives you a clear picture of where your money should go every month, helping you make the most of every dollar. Here are some ways to create and stick to a realistic budget:

- **Track your spending**: For a set period of time—say, a week or a month—write down everything you spend money on. This will give you a clear idea of where your money is going.
- **Categorize your expenses**: Divide your spending into categories like savings, essentials (food, clothes), and extras (games, outings).
- **Allocate wisely**: Based on your tracking, decide how much money to put into each category. Be realistic about your needs and consistent with your savings goals.

- **Review regularly**: At the end of each month, review your spending. Did you stick to your budget? Where could you improve? Adjust your budget as needed.

Remember, a budget doesn't restrict freedom. It's a tool that helps you achieve your financial goals while still enjoying life.

Delayed Gratification

Delayed gratification is a cornerstone of financial discipline. It's choosing to wait for a more significant reward instead of giving in to the temptation of immediate pleasure. Here's why it's worth practicing:

- **Bigger and better rewards**: Saving for a bigger goal often means the reward is much more satisfying than smaller impulse purchases.
- **Reduced buyer's remorse**: Waiting to make a purchase often leads to more thoughtful spending, reducing the chances of regretting your decisions later.
- **Increased financial stability**: Practicing delayed gratification helps you save more, spend less, and avoid debt, leading to a more stable financial future.

Learning to wait for what you want can be as simple as picking something you'd like to save for, and then slowly saving money until you can buy it. Each time you choose to save instead of spend, you're reinforcing the habit of delayed gratification.

Financial discipline might sound daunting, but it's really just making choices that align with your goals. It allows you to see the big picture and understand that the best rewards are often those we work hard for and wait patiently to achieve. Every time you make a smart choice with your money, you're not just saving, you're creating a base for a future where you can achieve your money goals and make your dreams come true, one smart step at a time.

7.4 ASKING FOR HELP: WHEN TO TALK TO ADULTS ABOUT MONEY

Money talks can sometimes feel like trying to understand a foreign language. That's okay, though. Everyone starts somewhere, and asking questions is how we learn and grow. Imagine cracking open a secret code with the help of those who've been decoding it for years. That's what talking about money with adults can feel like—unlocking secrets that make managing money easier and more effective.

Opening Up Conversations

Starting a conversation about money might seem hard, but it's like ripping off a band-aid. The initial hesitation quickly gives way to relief once you dive in. Trusted adults in your life—be it parents, older siblings, or family friends—have a treasure trove of experiences. They've likely faced money challenges and triumphs and can share wisdom you won't find in any textbook. Try asking them about their first savings goal or what they wish they knew about money when they were your age. You'll be surprised at how much you can learn from their stories.

Learning From Others

There's a saying that wisdom is learning from the mistakes of others. Your family, teachers, and even neighbors have all navigated their financial waters, sometimes smoothly, other times not so much. Their journeys are resources for you. Did your aunt invest in something that didn't pan out? What did she learn? Has a teacher ever shared a story about a financial blunder? These real-life lessons are invaluable. They give you the knowledge to make informed decisions and avoid similar pitfalls.

Seeking Professional Advice

Sometimes you might need more than just family wisdom, especially when you're planning for big goals like college. This is where financial advisors can be game-changers. Think of them as guides in the complex world of money management. They can help you understand saving options, the magic of compound interest, and how to start investing wisely, even with a small amount. If your family has a financial advisor, ask if you can join a meeting. Many banks and community centers also offer financial planning sessions. They're like having a coach for your money, helping you train to reach your financial fitness goals.

Resources for Learning

The great news is that more resources are available to you than ever. Websites and apps can make learning about money management both fun and engaging. Here are a few to get you started:

- Websites like Biz Kid$ offer a wealth of information, interactive games, and real-life stories of kids and money.
- Apps like Bankaroo for kids and teens offer a hands-on approach to managing virtual money, teaching valuable skills in a controlled environment.

Dip your toes into these resources. Each one has something unique to offer, from beginning concepts to advanced strategies, all tailored to help you navigate your financial journey.

As we wrap up this exploration into the world of money management, remember it's okay to ask for help. Whether it's opening up to trusted adults, learning from their experiences, seeking professional advice, or exploring online resources, every step you take builds your understanding and confidence in handling money. These conversations equip you with the tools to make informed decisions, set and achieve goals, and navigate the financial challenges and opportunities that lie ahead. Now, with a solid grasp of money management basics and the wisdom gleaned from those around you, you're ready to move forward, making smarter financial choices that pave the way to a bright and prosperous future.

CHAPTER 8
THE CLEAR GLASS: SEEING THROUGH MONEY MATTERS

I magine walking into a room full of windows. Some windows reveal a very clear picture, while others are cracked or dirty. The clear windows help you see where to go to avoid obstacles or wrong paths, while the cracked or dirty ones block your path. This is similar to being transparent in money matters. The clearer we are about our financial dealings, the easier it is to avoid problems like scams or dishonesty.

Transparency is the cornerstone of trust, especially when handling money. Whether within personal finance or the wider business world, being open about financial transactions and decisions can build bridges of trust. Yet the fog of scams and the allure of easy gains can sometimes cloud our judgment. Here's how to keep your financial dealings as transparent as those clear windows so you can always see the way forward.

8.1 UNDERSTANDING FINANCIAL TRANSPARENCY

Financial transparency means keeping the curtains open on all your money dealings. It means making sure everything from your savings progress to your spending habits is visible, not just to you but also to anyone else involved, like parents or financial advisors. In businesses, it involves openly sharing financial reports and operations with stakeholders.

Financial transparency is important because it builds trust. When people can see where their money is going or how a business operates financially, it fosters confidence and security. It clears up suspicion and doubt, making financial relationships smoother and more straightforward.

Honesty With Money

Being honest about money, whether with yourself, your family, or in any financial transaction, is a key part of transparency. This means:

- **Paying what you owe**: Paying back any money you borrow from friends or family on time shows you are trustworthy and honest.
- **Full disclosure**: When you borrow or lend money, it's important to be clear about how much you have, and how you'll either pay it back or be paid back. Talking about how much extra money (interest) needs to be paid, how and when the money will be returned, and if there are any money problems right from the start helps avoid confusion and builds trust.

Teaching Transparency

For parents and educators, instilling the value of transparency in young minds is crucial. It paves the way for responsible and trustworthy financial behaviors in the future. Here's how to make it part of everyday learning:

- **Be an open book**: Share your financial decisions, the reasoning behind them, and their outcomes with your kids. Let them in on the process, whether it's about budgeting for groceries or choosing a savings account.
- **Encourage questions**: Foster an environment where asking about money matters is okay. Talk about how credit cards work or why we pay taxes, providing clear, honest answers that demystify financial concepts.
- **Lead by example**: Practice what you preach. Let your kids see you reviewing bills, discussing finances openly with your partner, or researching before making an investment. Actions often speak louder than words.

8.2 FINANCIAL SCAMS: STAYING SAFE AND SMART

These days, pocket money can be sent with a click and piggy banks are getting smart, and the shadows of financial scams loom larger and sneakier than ever. From the age-old bait of prize-winning emails to the more sophisticated online identity thefts, scams have evolved, preying on the internet's uninformed and overly trusting souls.

Overview of Common Financial Scams

Scams are like the chameleons of the financial world. They blend in, adapting to the latest trends and technologies to catch you off guard. Young folks and adults alike might find themselves facing:

- **Phishing emails and messages**: These trick you into giving away personal info under the guise of legitimate requests from banks or familiar services.
- **Fake online stores**: Ever stumbled upon a sale too good to ignore? Some of these are fronts for collecting payment details without delivering the goods.
- **Investment fraud**: Offers promising you'll make lots of money with little to no risk might lead you down a path where the only thing growing is the scammer's wallet.
- **Identity theft**: A scary scenario where someone steals your personal information and then uses it to steal your money or commit other crimes, leaving you to untangle the mess.

Here are some red flags to watch for:

1. **Pressure to act quickly**: Scammers often create a sense of urgency, pushing you to make decisions on the spot without giving you time to think or consult others.
2. **Requests for personal or financial information**: Be cautious if you're asked for sensitive details like your bank account numbers, Social Security number, or login credentials for online accounts. No responsible company asks for your password in an email.
3. **Unsolicited contact**: Receiving unexpected calls, emails, or messages, especially from unknown sources or pretending to be from a real organization, can be a scam attempt.

4. **Too good to be true offers**: Promises of high returns with no risk, winning a contest you didn't enter, or deals that seem too good to be true are classic scam tactics.
5. **Payment requests via unusual methods**: Scammers often ask for payments through wire transfers, prepaid debit cards, gift cards, or cryptocurrencies, which are hard to trace and recover.
6. **Vague details and lack of transparency**: If the person or organization is vague about who they are, where they are located, or details of the offer, that's a red flag telling you to check with an adult before continuing.
7. **Spelling and grammar errors**: Professional organizations usually have communications checked for errors, so poorly written emails or messages can be a sign of a scam.
8. **Mismatched email addresses or URLs**: If the email address or link doesn't match the supposed organization's official domain, it could be a phishing attempt.
9. **Asking to keep transactions a secret**: Scammers might ask you not to tell anyone about the deal, aiming to isolate you from advice that could reveal the scam.
10. **Manipulation tactics**: Emotional manipulation, such as creating fear (e.g., claiming you'll be arrested for unpaid taxes) or offering sympathy or friendship, is often used to exploit victims.

Protecting Personal Information

The key to keeping scammers at bay is to treat your personal and financial information like the crown jewels—keep them under lock and key. Here are some ways to stay safe:

- **Strong passwords**: Use a mix of letters, numbers, and symbols that are hard to guess. Have a parent help you keep track of them all.
- **Privacy settings**: On social media, lock your profiles. The less strangers know about you, the better.
- **Secure connections**: Public Wi-Fi can be a hacker's playground. Avoid accessing sensitive accounts when connected to them.
- **Shred and secure**: Old-fashioned paper can still hold valuable info. Shred documents you don't need and keep important ones in a safe place.

Critical Thinking

If your gut says something's fishy, it probably is. Scammers love to create a sense of urgency or excitement to cloud your judgment. Slow down and think.

- **Question everything**: Why would your bank email you asking for your password? Can that online investment really guarantee high returns with no risk?
- **Research**: A quick internet search can reveal if others have encountered similar scams.
- **Talk about it**: Sometimes just discussing a suspicious offer with someone else can highlight its absurdity.

Reporting and Recovery

So you've spotted a scam or, worse, fallen for one. It's not the end of the world, but action is needed:

- **Report it**: Have a parent help you. Banks, social media platforms, and government agencies have channels for reporting fraud. They can also offer guidance on your next steps.
- **Change passwords**: If your information might have been compromised, change your passwords immediately.
- **Monitor your accounts**: Regularly check your bank account and credit report for any unusual activity.
- **Learn from it**: Every scam faced is a lesson learned. Share your experience to help protect others.

In every tale of heroes and villains, knowledge is power. By staying informed about the types of scams out there, keeping your personal and financial information safe, thinking critically, and knowing how to react if things go bad, you're not just protecting your money but building a fortress around your financial future. Now, let's move forward to the next chapter, ready to take on the exciting financial adventures ahead.

8.3 FINANCIAL HONESTY QUIZ

Try this fun, interactive quiz that tests your knowledge on financial transparency, covering topics like recognizing scams, the importance of honesty in money dealings, and ways to maintain financial integrity. Each question comes with feedback to help reinforce learning.

Question 1: What should you do if a stranger online asks for your parent's bank account details to give you a free video game?

    A. Give them the details.
    B. Ignore the request.
    C. Ask for two video games instead.
    D. Tell a trusted adult about it.

Feedback: Answer D. Great choice! If someone you don't know asks for private information, you should always tell a trusted adult. Scammers often use tricks like this to steal money.

Question 2: Why is it important to tell the truth when talking about how much allowance you have?

A. It makes you more popular.
B. It helps build trust with others.
C. You get more allowance.
D. It's not that important.

Feedback: Answer B. Correct! Being honest about your money builds trust, and people will know they can rely on you to be truthful.

Question 3: If a friend lends you money to buy a toy, what's the best way to handle it?

A. Pay them back as promised.
B. Wait for them to forget about it.
C. Tell them you lost the money.
D. Buy them a gift instead.

Feedback: Answer A. Exactly right! Paying back money you owe shows you respect your friend and take your promises seriously.

Question 4: What is a scam?

A. A type of dance.
B. A trick to steal your money.
C. A new video game.
D. A financial advisor.

Feedback: Answer B. Spot on! A scam is a trick someone uses to steal money or information. Always be cautious and ask an adult if something seems suspicious.

Question 5: If you see an ad promising free money, what should you think?

A. It's my lucky day!
B. It might be a scam.
C. I should click on it immediately.
D. I should tell all my friends.

Feedback: Answer B. Well done! Offers of free money are usually too good to be true and could be scams. Always check with an adult before responding.

Question 6: Why is it important to discuss the details when borrowing or lending money with a friend?

A. It's not really important.
B. To make the conversation longer.
C. To prevent misunderstandings and keep the friendship strong.
D. To confuse everyone.

Feedback: Answer C. Absolutely! Discussing details like when you'll pay them back helps avoid any confusion and keeps your friendship healthy and happy.

Question 7: What should you do before making a deal or trade, like swapping toys with a friend?

A. Talk about it clearly and agree on the details.
B. Just go ahead and swap without talking.
C. Make the trade secretly.
D. Change your mind at the last minute.

Feedback: Answer A. Great job! Talking things over and agreeing on the details first makes sure both friends are happy and there are no surprises.

Question 8: How can you be financially transparent or completely honest with your parents about your allowance?

A. Only tell them about what you save.
B. Share how you plan to spend and save, and any mistakes you've made.
C. Hide some of your spending.
D. Spend it all quickly so there's nothing to tell.

Feedback: Answer B. That's the way! Being open with your parents about your money helps you learn and grow, and they can offer great advice and support.

Checklist for Transparent Financial Dealings

- Always research before investing or engaging in financial opportunities.
- Keep records of all transactions, big or small.
- Discuss financial decisions openly with family members or advisors.
- Regularly review your financial habits and goals, keeping an eye out for areas to improve transparency.
- Educate yourself and others about the dangers of scams and the importance of honesty in all financial matters.

In a world where financial dealings can sometimes feel like navigating a maze of mirrors, choosing transparency is like carrying a light that reveals the true path. It guides your way and illuminates the road for those following in your footsteps. By committing to clear, honest, and open financial practices, we can all contribute to a future where trust and integrity lead the way in personal finance and beyond.

CHAPTER 9
MONEY MAGIC: TRANSFORMING FINANCE WITH FUN AND GAMES

I magine you're at a magic show where the magician pulls a rabbit out of a hat, makes coins disappear, and then, with a flourish, turns those same coins into a shower of colorful paper money. What if I told you that you could perform your own kind of magic right at home, transforming how you think about and handle money, all while having a blast? Yes, you heard that right! This chapter is all about turning financial literacy into an exciting game, one that not only educates but entertains. From board games that mimic real-life financial situations to creating your very own game that teaches you the ropes of economics, we will explore how fun and finance can go hand in hand.

9.1 BOARD GAMES THAT TEACH FINANCIAL LITERACY

Educational Value of Board Games

Board games have an incredible ability to teach concepts that may be complex in a fun and engaging way. Think about it. When trying to conquer a game, you're not just focused on winning, you're learning strategies, making decisions, and sometimes even doing a bit of math. And when it comes to financial literacy, board games can be a gold mine. They can show you the importance of saving, the impact of investments, and the consequences of debt, all within the confines of a game board. Plus, they bring people together, sparking conversations about money that might not happen otherwise.

Popular Financial Board Games

Some board games are classics for a reason. They've been around for ages and are still as popular as ever. Here's why:

- **Monopoly**: This game is practically a rite of passage. You're getting a crash course in real estate and money management as you buy properties, pay rent, and manage your cash. The key takeaway? Investing wisely can make you rich, but overextend yourself, and you could go bankrupt.
- **The Game of Life**: Here you're navigating life's big financial milestones—college, career, child-rearing, home buying, and retirement. It's a vivid reminder that our choices, especially financial ones, steer our life's direction.
- **Payday**: Living from paycheck to paycheck? Payday puts you in this scenario, teaching you to budget your monthly

income to cover bills and unexpected expenses and save a bit, too.

- **Cashflow**: Created by financial guru Robert Kiyosaki, it challenges players to get out of the rat race and onto the fast track, where their wealth can grow.

Creating Your Own Financial Board Game

Now, for the ultimate challenge: making your own board game. Why not turn what you've learned about earning, spending, saving, and investing into a game? You could design a game where players have to make money last through the month, invest in businesses, or save for retirement. The sky's the limit. Not only does this flex your creative muscles, but it also deepens your understanding of financial concepts. And who knows? Your game could become the next family favorite, teaching and entertaining players for generations to come.

Learning Through Competition

There's something about a little friendly competition that makes any game more thrilling. When you're competing, you're more focused, engaged, and determined to win. In the context of financial board games, this competition can simulate real-life financial decision-making and risk-taking. You could read about the stock market, but it's more fun to watch your investment in GameStop soar or plummet in a game, feeling that rush of excitement or pang of disappointment. This hands-on experience, even in a simulated environment, can prepare you for the ups and downs of real-world finances.

So grab a board game or start brainstorming your own, and dive into the world of financial literacy. Remember, the goal isn't just to win the game but to uncover hidden financial strategies and lessons, making you a better player and a smarter financial thinker.

9.2 FUN MONEY CHALLENGES FOR FAMILIES

Gather around, family! It's time to put a spin on our usual routines and add a sprinkle of excitement to our financial habits. Who said managing money had to be all spreadsheets and no play? Let's dive into some family-friendly challenges that will not only bring us closer but also teach us valuable lessons about money.

Saving Challenge

Imagine a treasure chest where every family member contributes, with eyes on a prize that benefits everyone. Sounds like an adventure, doesn't it? Here's the plan: We pick a goal that gets everyone pumped —maybe a new gaming console or a weekend getaway. Each week, we all chip in an agreed amount into our family treasure chest (a.k.a.

savings jar). Watching our collective treasure grow brings a sense of teamwork and anticipation. The best part? Reaching our goal and celebrating together, knowing we all played a part in achieving it.

Tips for success:

- Set a visible savings jar in a common area to remind and motivate everyone.
- Keep track of contributions with a colorful chart on the fridge.
- Encourage extra contributions by offering small, fun incentives, like choosing the next family movie night film.

Spending Diary

Let's turn into financial detectives for one week and track where our money goes. Everyone gets a notebook to write down their spending, no matter how small. At the end of the week, we'll have a family meeting to share our findings. This isn't about pointing fingers but understanding our spending patterns and thinking of ways to improve. Perhaps we'll discover that those small snack purchases add up or find expenses we can cut down on. It's all about gaining insights into our personal spending habits and brainstorming ways to be smarter with our money.

Tips for success:

- Encourage honesty and openness. There's no shame in any spending habits. It's all about learning.
- Highlight positive spending behaviors and suggest ways to support each other in making better choices.

Investment Simulation

Ready to play the stock market without the risk? Let's set up a family investment challenge using fake money. We can use an online stock market simulator or create our own with play money and a list of companies we're interested in. Each family member gets a set amount to pretend invest in stocks they choose. Over a month, track the performance of those investments, learning about the stock market's ups and downs. This challenge demystifies investing and teaches us the value of research and patience when growing our money.

Tips for success:

- Use real-life companies that everyone is familiar with to spark interest.
- Schedule weekly "family board meetings" to discuss investment strategies and what we've learned about the stock market.

Budgeting Challenge

Who can make their money last the longest while still covering all their needs? This challenge is all about stretching our dollars and understanding the importance of budgeting. Each family member plans a budget with their allocated money for the week, including expenses such as snacks, entertainment, and savings. The goal is to meet all our needs without running out of money. It's a practical, hands-on way to learn about prioritizing spending and the satisfaction of making smart financial choices.

Tips for success:

- Provide a list of common expenses to help everyone plan their budget.
- Encourage creativity in finding ways to save money, like eating homemade snacks instead of store-bought.
- Share budgeting tips and tricks at the end of the challenge to help each other improve.

These challenges are stepping stones toward building strong financial habits that will serve us well into the future. Plus, embarking on these adventures as a family makes the journey more enjoyable and strengthens our bond as we work together toward common goals. So let's dive in and add a dash of fun to our financial learning.

9.3 CREATIVE SAVINGS PROJECTS: DIY PIGGY BANKS

Saving money turns into an adventure when you can see your progress. It's like playing a video game where every coin saved gets you closer to unlocking a new level or a coveted item. This thrill is what makes visual savings aids so powerful. They transform the abstract concept of saving into something tangible, something you can see and feel. And what better way to kickstart this visual savings journey than with a DIY project?

Making Saving Visual

Imagine your savings as a colorful progress bar in a game, filling up slowly as you move closer to your goal. This is the magic of visual savings aids. They give your goals shape and color, making the act of saving more immediate and rewarding. Each coin or bill saved becomes a visual reminder of your progress, keeping motivation high and the end goal in sight.

DIY Piggy Banks

Let's roll up our sleeves and create our own piggy banks. You don't need fancy materials. Most of what you need is probably lying around the house.

- **Balloon and papier-mâché piggy bank**: Start with a balloon as your base, and layer strips of newspaper soaked in a glue and water mixture to create papier-mâché. Once dry, pop the balloon, paint the newspaper, and there you have it —a custom-made piggy bank. Cut a slot for money, and maybe craft a cork or papier-mâché stopper for the bottom.
- **Recycled bottle bank**: Take a clean plastic bottle, cut a money slot, and let your creativity loose with paints, stickers, or glitter. It's a great way to reuse and recycle, turning waste into a treasure chest.
- **Shadow box savings frame**: Transform a shadow box frame into a piggy bank with a purpose. Decorate the background with your savings goal, such as a picture of a bicycle, a game console, or a travel destination. Cut a slot on top for money. As you add money, you can watch your savings cover the picture until it fully disappears, providing you a clear visual goal.

Customizing Savings Goals

Personalizing your piggy banks connects you more deeply with your savings goals. It's like naming your character in a game; it makes the journey more personal. Here are some ideas:

- **Goal stickers**: Use stickers or draw directly on your piggy bank to represent your savings goal. If it's a new bike, how about some bike stickers? If it's a trip, maybe some travel icons or destinations.
- **Color coding**: Assign different colors to different goals. If you're saving for a concert ticket, you could paint your piggy bank in the artist's album colors or use the concert theme.
- **Savings tracker**: Attach a small chart or tracker to your piggy bank where you can mark your progress. Moving a clip or filling in a bar as you save can be incredibly satisfying.

9.4 FINANCIAL LITERACY MOVIE NIGHT: LEARNING FROM FILMS

Grab some popcorn and dim the lights—it's time for a movie night with a twist! Movies have a way of sticking with us, their stories and characters lingering long after the credits roll. But did you know they can also teach us valuable lessons about handling money? From documentaries that unravel the mysteries of the stock market to animated adventures with hidden economic lessons, films can be a fun and effective way to boost your financial smarts.

Educational Films on Finance

Movies and documentaries are fantastic tools for understanding complex topics like economics and personal finance. Here are a few that families can enjoy together:

- *The Secret Millionaire's Club* (2009): An animated series where Warren Buffett mentors a group of kids in making wise financial decisions and starting their own business ventures. It's both educational and entertaining, covering basic principles of economics and entrepreneurship.

- *Money Smart for Young People*: A series of videos developed by the FDIC that offers lessons in financial literacy for various age groups, including young children. These videos cover topics like saving, budgeting, and the importance of making smart financial decisions.
- *Biz Kid$* (2008): This Emmy Award-winning educational show teaches kids about money management and entrepreneurship. Each episode covers a different financial topic through real-life stories of young entrepreneurs and practical advice from experts.
- *Finance 101*: Money Management for Kids (YouTube Series): Various YouTube channels offer series tailored to teaching kids about finance. These videos can range from explaining basic concepts of money, saving tips, understanding the value of money, and introductory lessons on investing.
- *The Tooth Fairy* (2010) (PG): While not strictly educational, this family comedy starring Dwayne "The Rock" Johnson can be used to introduce discussions about money with younger children, such as the concept of the tooth fairy and the value of a dollar.
- *The Boy Who Harnessed the Wind* (2019) (PG): This inspirational film shows how innovation and determination can lead to creating solutions that improve communities. It can be used to discuss the value of resources, investment in education, and sustainable development.
- *Once Upon a Dime* (1949): Though older, this animated short film by the Federal Reserve Bank of New York explains how money was invented, the importance of savings, and how banks lend money. It's a timeless piece that simplifies complex concepts.

- *WALL-E* (G): At first glance, it's a story about robots and love, but it's also a commentary on consumerism, sustainability, and corporate monopolies.
- *Inside Job* (PG-13): This documentary provides a detailed analysis of the factors leading to the 2008 financial crisis. Best suited for older kids, it's a thorough backgrounder on economic policies and practices.

Watching these films can open up a world of discussion about financial principles, ethics, and the impact of economic decisions on the wider world.

Creating a Movie Log

Keep the learning going by starting a movie log. This can be a simple notebook or a digital document where you list:

- The films you've watched together.
- Key financial concepts or lessons each film covered.
- Personal reflections on the film's message and how it applies to your financial situation or goals.

This log serves as a living document of your financial education journey through films. It's a place to reflect on what you've learned and how you've grown in your understanding of money matters. Plus, it can be a great resource to revisit as you encounter new financial decisions or challenges.

The magic of movies lies in their ability to teach, inspire, and entertain all at once. By incorporating films into your financial literacy efforts, you're not just learning about money, you're experiencing stories that bring those lessons to life in vivid, memorable ways. This approach to financial education proves that learning about money doesn't have to be dull or daunting. With a little creativity, it can be as engaging and enjoyable as a movie night with your favorite snacks and people.

As we wrap up our exploration of financial literacy through fun and games, remember the key takeaway: Learning about money management can and should be an enjoyable experience. Whether it's through board games, family challenges, creative projects, or movie nights, there are countless ways to engage with financial concepts outside of textbooks and classrooms. These activities teach valuable lessons and foster discussions, creativity, and bonding among family members. So keep the popcorn popping, the dice rolling, and the conversations flowing as you continue on your path to financial savvy. Now, let's turn the page and discover new adventures in the next chapter, ready to build on our understanding and dive deeper into the world of personal finance.

CHAPTER 10
THE ART OF NEGOTIATION: YOUR FINANCIAL SUPERPOWER

Picture yourself at a garage sale. You spot a vintage skateboard, the kind you've seen in movies but never up close. The price tag reads more than you have in your pocket, but you feel a tug in your heart. It has to be yours. Now, what if I told you that with a bit of talking and a sprinkle of charm, you might skate away with it for less than the sticker price? That's right, we're talking about negotiation, a skill as valuable as any coin in your piggy bank.

Negotiation isn't just for business moguls in suits. It's a daily part of life, from deciding who gets the last slice of pepperoni pizza to convincing your parents why you deserve a bigger allowance. When it comes to money, knowing how to negotiate can save you a few bucks and teach you important lessons about value, communication, and compromise.

Basic Negotiation Principles

The foundation of any good negotiation lies in understanding its core principles. At its heart, negotiation is a conversation aimed at reaching an agreement where both parties feel valued and satisfied. Here's the kicker: It's not about winning or getting a one-up on the other person. Instead, it's about finding common ground and crafting a deal that benefits everyone involved. Remember, the best deals are those where everyone walks away happy.

Role-Playing Scenarios

One of the best ways to sharpen your negotiation skills is through role-playing. Why not grab a friend or family member and practice? You could simulate buying a car, setting up a lemonade stand, or even negotiating which movie to watch on family night. Through role-playing, you:

- learn how to think on your feet.
- get comfortable with back-and-forth dialogue.
- discover the importance of listening and adjusting your strategy based on what the other person says.

Negotiation Tactics

Armed with an understanding of negotiation's core principles and some practice under your belt, it's time to dive into tactics that can help swing things in your favor:

- **Research is your best friend**: Always go into a negotiation well-informed. Knowing the value of what you're negotiating for can give you the upper hand.
- **Ask open-ended questions**: These require more than just a yes or no answer, encouraging the other person to share more information, which you can use to your advantage.
- **Be ready to walk away**: Sometimes, the best deal is the one you don't make. If it doesn't feel right, be prepared to walk

away. This shows you're not desperate, often bringing the other party back to the table with a better offer.

Ethical Considerations

In every negotiation, integrity matters. It's easy to get caught up in the moment, stretch the truth, or make promises you can't keep. Here's the thing: Honesty and transparency lead to fairer outcomes and build your reputation as someone who is trustworthy. So always negotiate with ethics at the forefront. Remember, a good deal today based on dishonesty can lead to lost opportunities tomorrow.

Interactive Element: Negotiation Practice Journal

As always, writing about your experiences helps you understand what happened and notice trends that were successful and those that weren't. Use a journal with prompts designed to reflect on your negotiation experiences. In each entry, detail:

- the scenario that led to the negotiations.
- the tactics you used and their effectiveness.
- lessons learned and areas for improvement.

This journal becomes a personal playbook, helping you refine your negotiation skills over time.

Negotiation is like a dance. It takes two to tango, and knowing the steps can make the difference between stepping on toes and gliding gracefully across the floor. Whether you're haggling at a yard sale, debating chores and allowances, or navigating the bigger financial decisions that life throws your way, negotiation is a superpower worth developing. It teaches you about value, respect, and the art of compromise. So the next time you find yourself eyeing that vintage skateboard or any other treasure, remember, a little negotiation can go a long way.

10.2 NEGOTIATING ALLOWANCES: A GUIDE FOR KIDS AND PARENTS

Negotiating an allowance is a dance between kids and parents, a way to understand each other's perspectives and reach a happy middle ground. Here's how to make sure both sides come out feeling good about the agreement.

Setting the Stage

Before even thinking about sitting down to discuss allowances, both parents and kids must do a bit of homework.

- **Parents**: Consider what chores are being done and whether you believe your child could handle additional responsibilities. Reflect on the purpose of the allowance: Is it for teaching money management, rewarding hard work, or both?
- **Kids**: Think about what you currently contribute to the household and whether there's more you could do. Also, understand why you want or need an increase. Is it to save for something specific, cover more of your personal expenses, or something else?

A clear understanding of these points sets a solid foundation for a productive conversation.

Presenting Your Case

When it's time to negotiate, presenting your case clearly and confidently makes all the difference.

- **Be prepared**: Come to the table with a list of your current chores, responsibilities, and ideas for additional tasks you're willing to take on.
- **Know your "why"**: Be ready to explain why you're asking for more money. Whether it's saving for a new bike or wanting to manage more of your own spending, your reasons should be clear and reasonable.
- **Stay calm and respectful**: Even if the conversation doesn't go your way immediately, keeping a level head shows maturity. Remember, this is a discussion, not a demand.

Reaching an Agreement

Finding common ground is the goal. Here's how to navigate toward a deal that feels fair to everyone.

- **Listen**: Both sides should be open to hearing each other out. Parents might have valuable insights on budgeting and saving, while kids can share their perspectives on the value of their work and financial needs.
- **Compromise**: Maybe the exact amount you were hoping for isn't feasible, but there could be room for compromise. Additional chores could lead to a bonus, or there might be other ways to earn through special projects.
- **Consider increments**: Rather than a big bump all at once, suggest gradual increases tied to taking on more responsibilities. This approach allows for growth and adjustment over time.

Written Agreements

Putting things in writing clarifies expectations and commitments from both sides.

- **Outline responsibilities and rewards**: Clearly state what chores are expected and what the allowance will be. Include any conditions, like quality of work or completion deadlines.
- **Include opportunities for review**: Set dates to revisit the agreement. This could be every few months or tied to school terms. It's a chance to discuss what's working, what isn't, and whether any adjustments are needed.
- **Sign it together**: Having both parent and child sign the agreement solidifies the commitment. It's a physical

reminder of the conversation and the promises made by both parties.

Negotiating an allowance is about more than just money. It's a learning experience that involves understanding value, articulating needs and wants, and working together to find solutions. For kids, it's a step toward financial literacy and independence, grounded in real-life practice of negotiation and compromise. For parents, it's an opportunity to guide and support your child's growth, encouraging responsibility and smart money management.

10.3 BARGAIN HUNTING: HOW TO GET THE BEST DEALS

Shopping smart doesn't just keep your wallet happy. It's like a game where the prize is getting more bang for your buck. Whether you're scouting the local yard sale for a hidden gem or navigating the vast ocean of online shopping, snagging a great deal feels like winning a treasure hunt. Let's unlock some secrets to becoming a savvy shopper, ensuring you always bag the best deals.

Researching Prices

Start your quest for the perfect bargain by doing a bit of detective work. Before you commit to buying anything, take a moment to look around. The internet has several comparison tools and websites that are user-friendly enough for kids and allow you to see how prices stack up across different stores. Be sure to ask a trusted adult for some help and watch out for scams. Below are some options known for their reliability and simplicity.

1. **Google Shopping**: Google Shopping is a straightforward tool that allows users to compare prices for products across different retailers. It's user-friendly and provides a broad range of products, making it a great starting point for kids under supervision.
2. **ShopSavvy**: ShopSavvy is an app that lets users scan barcodes or search for products to find the best prices online and in-store. Its simple interface can be navigated easily with a little guidance, making it suitable for older kids.
3. **Honey**: Honey is a browser extension that automatically finds and applies coupon codes at checkout but also offers a price comparison tool. While it's more about saving than comparing, it does provide price history charts and alerts for price drops, which can be educational for kids to learn about timing their purchases.
4. **CamelCamelCamel**: Specifically for Amazon products, CamelCamelCamel offers price history charts and price drop alerts. It's a web-based tool that's easy to use and can

help kids learn about price trends and the best times
to buy.

5. **PriceGrabber**: PriceGrabber provides a comprehensive
platform for comparing prices across various products and
retailers. It's detailed and offers extensive search filters that
can help teach kids about making informed purchasing
decisions.

While these tools can save you a lot of moolah, it's important to have
a parent or trusted adult supervise your use of these apps and
websites. Never make purchases without parental consent and always
protect your personal information online!

Timing Purchases

Timing is everything, and that couldn't be more true than when
you're shopping. Ever notice how swimsuits are a steal in winter or
how holiday decorations are practically given away in January? That's
because off-season shopping can lead to some serious savings.
Retailers need to clear out old stock to make room for new arrivals,
which means discounts for you. If you can wait a bit to buy that new
skateboard or winter coat, timing your purchase right can lead to big
savings.

- Buy off-season items for the next year.
- Keep an eye on holiday sales and end-of-season clearances.
- Ask your parent if you can subscribe to store newsletters to
  get a heads-up on upcoming sales.

Haggling Tips

Haggling may seem old-school, but it's an art that can still save you
some serious cash, especially at yard sales, flea markets, and even some

retail stores that are willing to match prices of other stores. The key is to be polite and reasonable. No one likes a pushy haggler. Start by expressing genuine interest in the item, then ask if the price is negotiable. Sometimes, just by asking, you'll get a better deal. And if you're buying multiple items, see if there's a discount for bundling them together. Remember, the worst they can say is no, but the best? You walk away with a great deal and a story to tell.

- Always be polite and respectful when haggling.
- Suggest a fair price that's lower than what you're willing to pay, giving you some room to meet in the middle.
- If the seller can't lower the price, see if they can throw in something extra to sweeten the deal.

10.4 CONFLICT RESOLUTION: MONEY AND FRIENDSHIPS

When money mixes with friendships, the blend can sometimes turn bittersweet. It's not uncommon for pals to find themselves in a pickle over unpaid loans or differing opinions on joint spending. But here's the good news: Navigating these choppy waters doesn't have to spell disaster for your relationships. With the right approach, resolving financial disagreements can actually strengthen bonds, proving that friendships can flourish even when money matters get complicated.

Money conflicts among friends often sprout from situations like one friend not paying back a loan on time or squabbling over splitting the cost of something you want to buy together. These moments, though small, can test the fabric of your friendship. Yet they also offer a chance for growth, teaching valuable lessons about empathy, understanding, and the importance of talking things through.

Speaking of talking it out, that is the golden key to resolving financial disagreements. Here's a simple truth: Most conflicts are born from misunderstandings, and a calm, honest chat can clear up confusion. When a money issue arises:

- Start the conversation with how you feel, using "I" statements to avoid placing blame. ("I feel confused because you said you would pay me, but you haven't.")
- Listen actively, giving your friend space to share their side of the story.
- Aim to understand their viewpoint, even if you don't entirely agree.

Think of solving problems with friends like playing a team sport. Fairness and compromise are the key players that make sure everyone wins. Sometimes, when you're trying to decide what to do together, not everyone will agree right away. You might want to go big—like buying the coolest, most expensive gift for a friend's birthday. But what if one of your teammates doesn't have enough allowance to pitch in?

Instead of sticking to the original plan and leaving someone out, you could come up with a new game plan. Maybe find a gift that's just as awesome but doesn't cost as much, or think of other ways your friend could help, like planning a surprise birthday game or making a homemade card. This way, everyone gets to contribute in their own way, and no one feels left out. The game is fun and fair for everyone —and that's how you score a true friendship win.

Setting clear expectations and boundaries around money from the get-go can steer friendships clear of potential pitfalls. Here are a few ideas:

- When lending money, agree on repayment terms beforehand. A simple "Can you pay me back by the end of the month?" can set a clear expectation.

- For shared expenses, use apps that track and split costs transparently. This way, everyone knows who owes what, leaving little room for confusion.
- Have open conversations about financial comfort zones. Understanding each other's limits can prevent awkward situations where someone feels pressured to overspend.

Money doesn't have to be a wedge that drives friends apart. When tackled with care, honesty, and a dash of creativity, financial disagreements can be resolved in ways that actually reinforce trust and understanding. And remember, the true value of a friendship isn't measured in dollars and cents but in the support, laughter, and memories shared along the way.

Navigating money matters with friends can certainly test the waters, but it doesn't have to capsize the ship. By fostering open communication, embracing fairness and compromise, and setting clear boundaries, these challenges can transform into opportunities for growth. Through this process, we learn about managing money and the invaluable skill of maintaining and strengthening our relationships. As we transition to the next chapter, we carry forward these lessons, ready to explore new dimensions of financial literacy and personal growth, always remembering the importance of empathy, respect, and understanding in every aspect of our lives.

CHAPTER 11
THE MONEY WIZARD'S PLAYBOOK

In a world where lemonade stands get upgraded to online stores and piggy banks turn digital, young minds are not just participating in the financial world, they're reshaping it. With fresh perspectives, they're solving old problems in new ways, proving that age is just a number when it comes to innovation. Let's take a closer look at how these young innovators are shaking things up and how you, too, might join this league of extraordinary thinkers.

Youth Financial Innovators

Imagine a teenager who's noticed how her friends struggle to save money. Instead of shrugging it off, she develops an app that rounds up their purchases to the nearest dollar, stashing the change away into a savings account. Or picture a group of kids who've started a recycling business, trading cans and bottles for cash and using the proceeds to fund community projects. These aren't just hypothetical scenarios. They're real stories of kids and teens identifying gaps and opportunities in their world and stepping in with solutions.

- Savings apps developed by teens for their peers focus on user-friendly design and gamification to make saving fun.
- Youth-led environmental businesses turn ecological action into economic opportunity by recycling or crafting eco-friendly products.

Their success lies not just in their ideas but in their approach. They see a need, imagine a way to fill it, and dare to try.

Encouraging Innovation

You might wonder, "How can I start thinking like an innovator?" Here are a few strategies:

- **Stay curious**: Ask questions about how things work and why. Often, innovation starts with a simple, "What if... ?"

- **Observe and listen**: Pay attention to conversations around you, especially complaints or wishes for "something better." These can be golden opportunities for innovation.
- **Learn by doing**: Don't be afraid to experiment. Whether it's coding a simple app or starting a small project, hands-on experience is invaluable.

Remember, every big breakthrough begins with a small step. The key is to start.

The Role of Mentorship

Behind many young innovators is a mentor, someone who's been there, done that, and is willing to guide you through the process of turning ideas into reality. Finding a mentor can:

- **Boost your confidence**: Sometimes, just knowing someone believes in you can push you to keep going.
- **Provide practical advice**: From technical skills to navigating challenges, mentors can offer insights you might not find anywhere else.
- **Expand your network**: Mentors often introduce you to others who can help, opening doors you didn't even know existed.

So, how do you find a mentor? Start by reaching out to teachers, family friends, or professionals in fields you're interested in. Be clear about what you hope to achieve with your mentor and why you think they'd be the right fit.

Future of Money: Predictions From Young Minds

In a world where piggy banks are becoming more virtual than actual and allowance transactions can happen with a quick tap on a screen, it's clear that the concept of money is evolving right before our eyes. Now imagine if we handed the crystal ball to the younger generation, the true digital natives. What kind of future financial landscape do they foresee?

Kids' Predictions

When we listen to kids' predictions about the future of money, their ideas range from wildly imaginative to eerily plausible. Some envision a world where cryptocurrencies are as common as cash once was, used to buy everything from a spaceship ride to candy at the corner store. Others foresee a shift toward a more barter-based system, leveraging technology to trade skills instead of currency. Imagine an app that lets you exchange piano lessons for coding classes. The common thread in these predictions is a move toward more personalized and direct exchanges of value facilitated by technology.

- Cryptocurrencies as common currency
- A resurgence of barter systems, enhanced by tech platforms

Learning From the Past

To truly appreciate these forward-looking visions, it's helpful to glance back at how money has changed over the centuries. From trading shells and salt to the introduction of paper money and then to plastic cards, each evolution was sparked by the need for more convenience and security. These historical shifts show us that while the form of money may change, its core purpose—to facilitate exchange—remains constant. This historical lens helps kids understand that their predictions aren't just fanciful dreams but part of an ongoing evolution.

The Impact of Technology

Technology's role in shaping our financial systems cannot be overstated. Kids today are growing up in an era where digital wallets are more common than physical ones. They see the potential for tech not just to change how we spend or save but to make financial systems more inclusive and accessible. For instance, imagine a world where blockchain technology ensures every child has access to a savings account from birth or where AI advisors help people make smarter spending decisions, leveling the playing field for financial literacy.

- Digital wallets becoming the norm
- Blockchain and AI as tools for financial inclusivity and literacy

Creative Envisioning

To harness these imaginative ideas, schools and communities are increasingly holding workshops and contests that challenge kids to design their versions of the future of finance. Kids articulate their visions through drawing, writing, or even building models, from money that grows on trees to accounts that automatically donate a percentage to charity. These activities spark creativity and give kids a sense of ownership over their future, encouraging them to think critically about the role of money in society and their lives.

- Workshops and contests for kids to design the future of finance
- Fostering a sense of ownership and critical thinking about money

As we wrap up this exploration into the future of money through the eyes of our youngest visionaries, it's clear that their ideas hold the seeds of possibility. They envision a world where money is not just a means of transaction but a tool for empowerment, creativity, and global connection. By listening to their predictions and understanding the historical journey of money, we're reminded that the essence of finance is always evolving, shaped by our collective needs, dreams, and innovations. As we turn the page, let's carry forward this sense of possibility and openness to change, ready to embrace whatever the future holds.

CONCLUSION

Well, folks, we've officially reached the treasure chest at the end of our grand financial literacy adventure. From the humble beginnings of understanding the almighty dollar (or whatever currency floats your boat) to the lofty ideals of saving, spending wisely, and investing like mini moguls. We've navigated the tricky waters of credit, dived into the digital dollars of the future, and even learned how to turn hobbies into cold, hard cash (or at least a steady trickle of digital currency).

Starting young on this journey gives you a head start and sets up a solid foundation for your financial house (which you're now more equipped to save for). The habits you've started forming, the knowledge you've soaked up like a sponge, and the attitude you've developed toward money are more precious than the contents of any piggy bank. They're the keys to a kingdom where your financial well-being reigns supreme.

Let's review the golden nuggets we've unearthed together:

- Save like a squirrel stashing nuts for the winter.
- Spend with the wisdom of a sage, not like a kid in a candy store.
- Invest with the curiosity of a cat but the caution of a turtle.
- Understand credit as if your superhero cape depended on it.
- Embrace the global economy like you're giving the world a giant bear hug.

And, in the spirit of breaking the mold, remember that creativity and innovation in managing your moolah can lead to some epic financial wins. Don't be afraid to unleash your inner financial wizard, leverage tech to make your money work smarter, not harder, and explore the entrepreneurial wilderness with gusto.

This is hardly the end, my young apprentices. It's merely the beginning of a lifelong quest for financial savvy. The world of finance is as vast and changing as the ocean, with new concepts to explore, technologies to harness, and strategies to master. Keep that curiosity alive, and never stop seeking knowledge and adventure in personal finance.

Now, I challenge you to take action. Start small, dream big, and celebrate every victory along the way. Whether it's setting up your first budget, opening a savings account, or investing in your first stock, every step forward is a step toward your financial independence.

Don't keep all this newfound wisdom to yourself. Share the wealth (of knowledge) with your family, friends, and even your loyal pet (hey, they might enjoy the sound of your voice). Teaching and discussing these topics reinforces your learning and can inspire those around you to start their own financial literacy journey.

I'm tipping my hat to you for embarking on this adventure. Your dedication to navigating the sometimes choppy, sometimes exhilarating waters of personal finance is nothing short of heroic. As you sail into the future, remember that your potential to make wise decisions and achieve financial success is as boundless as the sea. Envision a future where you are the captain of your financial destiny, steering toward your dreams with confidence and skill.

Here's to you, future financial champions. May your wallets be heavy, your hearts light, and your journey rich with learning and growth. Onward and upward!

PASSING THE TORCH OF FINANCIAL WISDOM

Congratulations, young savers and spenders! You've navigated through the twists and turns of The Ultimate Guide to Financial Literacy for Kids and emerged with a treasure trove of knowledge about money, saving, and investing. You're now equipped with the tools to carve out a path to financial success and security.

But as you stand at this exciting crossroads, with the power to make smart financial choices in your hands, there's one more quest that lies ahead. It's time to share the wealth of knowledge you've gained and light the way for others on their financial journey.

By leaving your honest review of this book on Amazon, you're not just sharing your thoughts but guiding future financial adventurers to the map that helped you discover the secrets of money management. Your review is a beacon, illuminating the path for others seeking guidance and inspiration to embark on their own quest for financial literacy.

Your voice matters, and your experience could be the key to unlocking a world of opportunity for someone else. By passing on your passion for financial literacy, you're contributing to a brighter future for all.

Thank you for being an integral part of keeping the spirit of financial education alive. Together, we're not just learning about money; we're building a community of informed, responsible, and empowered individuals.

Scan the QR code to share your journey and leave your review on Amazon.

https://www.amazon.com/review/create-review/?asin= B0CZDGZGFG

Your insight and enthusiasm are the sparks that can ignite a passion for financial literacy in others. By sharing your review, you're ensuring that the flame of knowledge burns brightly for generations to come.

Thank you for joining us on this adventure and helping spread the magic of financial literacy. Your contribution is invaluable; together, we're making a difference, one review at a time.

With gratitude, Your friends at Money Mentor Publications

REFERENCES

1. Bankrate. (n.d.). Investing basics for kids: How to teach children to save and invest. Retrieved from https://www.bankrate.com/investing/how-to-teach-kids-about-investing/

2. Big Life Journal. (n.d.). 7 Fun Goal-Setting Activities for Children. Retrieved from https://biglifejournal.com/blogs/blog/5-fun-goal-setting-activities-children

3. Britannica Kids. (n.d.). Sustainability - Kids | Britannica Kids | Homework Help. Retrieved from https://kids.britannica.com/kids/article/sustainability/631786

4. Business Insider. (2024, February). Best Investment Apps for Beginners in February 2024. Retrieved from https://www.businessinsider.com/personal-finance/best-investment-apps-for-beginners

5. Campbellsville University Online. (n.d.). Benefits of Financial Literacy for Kids. Retrieved from https://online.campbellsville.edu/education/financial-literacy-for-kids/

6. Carosa, C. (2021, May 22). True Stories Of Children Saving Successfully. Forbes. Retrieved from https://www.forbes.com/sites/chriscarosa/2021/05/22/true-stories-of-children-saving-successfully/

7. Clear, J. (n.d.). The Marshmallow Experiment and the Power of Delayed Gratification. Retrieved from https://jamesclear.com/delayed-gratification

8. CNN Money. (2015, April 28). Meet the 17-year-old investor who tripled his money. Retrieved from https://money.cnn.com/2015/04/28/investing/millennial-investor-17-year-old-brandon-fleisher/

9. Cool Crafts. (n.d.). 40 Cool DIY Piggy Banks For Kids & Adults. Retrieved from https://www.coolcrafts.com/cool-diy-piggy-banks/

10. Credit Canada. (n.d.). How Financial Technology is Changing the Way Kids Learn About Money. Retrieved from https://www.creditcanada.com/blog/how-financial-technology-is-changing-the-way-kids-learn-about-money

11. DebtConsolidationUSA. (n.d.). 6 Movies With Great Money Lessons For Kids. Retrieved from https://www.debtconsolidationusa.com/personal-finance/6-movies-great-money-lessons-kids.html

12. Ducksters. (n.d.). Money and Finance: History of Money. Retrieved from https://www.ducksters.com/money/history_of_money.php

13. ElementaryEdu. (2022, July). How to Teach The Difference Between Wants and Needs (11 Strategies). Retrieved from https://elementaryedu.com/2022/07/the-difference-between-wants-and-needs.html

14. Freedomsprout. (n.d.). 53 Board Games to Teach Your Kids About Money (At Every Age). Retrieved from https://freedomsprout.com/money-board-games/

15. GoHenry. (n.d.). 18 Fun Money Activities for Kids. Retrieved from https://www.gohenry.com/us/blog/financial-education/18-fun-money-activities-for-kids

16. GoHenry. (n.d.). Should you get a prepaid card for your kids? (pros + cons). Retrieved from https://www.gohenry.com/us/blog/financial-education/should-you-get-a-prepaid-card-for-your-kids

17. GoHenry. (n.d.). Teaching kids about credit in simple terms. Retrieved from https://www.gohenry.com/us/blog/financial-education/teaching-kids-about-credit-in-simple-terms

18. GoHenry. (n.d.). The 8 best budgeting & money apps for kids & teens. Retrieved from https://www.gohenry.com/uk/blog/financial-education/the-best-budgeting-apps-for-families

19. GoHenry. (n.d.). Teaching Your Child To Recognize and Avoid Internet Scams. Retrieved from https://www.gohenry.com/us/blog/online-safety/teaching-your-child-to-recognize-and-avoid-internet-scams

20. Good Housekeeping. (2002, November). Money Lessons for Kids. Retrieved from https://www.goodhousekeeping.com/life/money/advice/a12132/money-lessons-kids-nov02/

21. Investopedia. (n.d.). 10 Successful Young Entrepreneurs. Retrieved from https://www.investopedia.com/10-successful-young-entrepreneurs-4773310

22. Investopedia. (n.d.). How to Teach Your Child About Cryptocurrency. Retrieved from https://www.investopedia.com/how-to-teach-your-child-about-cryptocurrency-5224013

23. Investopedia. (n.d.). How to Teach Your Child About Investing. Retrieved from https://www.investopedia.com/articles/pf/07/childinvestor.asp

24. Kiplinger. (n.d.). My 10 Best Financial Literacy Apps for Kids. Retrieved from https://www.kiplinger.com/article/saving/t065-c032-s014-my-10-best-financial-literacy-apps-for-kids.html

25. LinkedIn. (n.d.). Negotiation Training Games: Fun and Effective Ways to Improve Your Skills. Retrieved from https://www.linkedin.com/pulse/negotiation-training-games-fun-effective-ways-improve

26. Money Geek. (n.d.). Money Foundations for Kids: Compound Interest. Retrieved from https://www.moneygeek.com/financial-planning/compound-interest-for-kids/

27. MoneySupermarket.com. (n.d.). How to teach kids to be ethical consumers as adults. Retrieved from https://www.moneysupermarket.com/news/how-to-teach-kids-to-be-ethical-consumers-as-adults

28. MyDoh. (n.d.). How to Help Kids and Teens Avoid Impulse Buying. Retrieved from https://www.mydoh.ca/learn/blog/lifestyle/how-to-help-kids-and-teens-avoid-impulse-buying/

29. MyDoh. (n.d.). How to Teach Your Kids Negotiation Skills. Retrieved from https://www.mydoh.ca/learn/blog/lifestyle/how-to-teach-your-kids-negotiation-skills/

30. MyDoh. (n.d.). 10 Money Mistakes Teens Make and How to Avoid Them. Retrieved from https://www.mydoh.ca/learn/blog/banking/10-money-mistakes-teens-make-and-how-to-avoid-them/

31. Partner Colorado Credit Union. (n.d.). How to Start a Financial Journal. Retrieved from https://www.partnercoloradocu.org/resources/financial-educa tion/savings/how-to-start-a-financial-journal

32. Pon Harvard Edu. (n.d.). Ethics and Negotiation: 5 Principles of Negotiation to Boost Your Bargaining Skills in Your Personal and Professional Life. Retrieved from https://www.pon.harvard.edu/daily/negotiation-training-daily/questions-of-ethics-in-negotiation/

33. QinPrinting. (n.d.). How to Design an Educational Board Game. Retrieved from https://www.qinprinting.com/blog/how-to-design-an-educational-board-game/

34. Quicken. (n.d.). 12 Fun Summer Money Challenges for Kids. Retrieved from https://www.quicken.com/blog/challenges-for-kids/

35. Ramsey Solutions. (n.d.). 15 Ways to Teach Kids About Money. Retrieved from https://www.ramseysolutions.com/relationships/how-to-teach-kids-about-money

36. Savvy Sparrow. (n.d.). 75 Rewards for Kids (and How to Make Rewards Work). Retrieved from https://thesavvysparrow.com/rewards-for-kids/

37. The Balance Money. (n.d.). Budgeting for Kids: How To Teach It and Why It Matters. Retrieved from https://www.thebalancemoney.com/teach-kids-to-budget-money-454012

38. Ameriprise Financial. (n.d.). Financial literacy for kids: Teaching kids about money. Retrieved from https://www.ameriprise.com/financial-goals-priorities/family-estate/6-simple-ways-to-raise-financially-savvy-kids

39. Bankaroo. (n.d.). 8 Tips for Keeping Your Kids Safe When Banking or Shopping Online. Retrieved from https://bankaroo.com/8-tips-for-keeping-your-kids-safe-when-banking-or-shopping-online/

40. Forbes Advisor. (n.d.). How To Open A Savings Account For A Child. Retrieved from https://www.forbes.com/advisor/banking/savings/guide-to-childrens-and-kids-savings-accounts/

41. ClassTechTips. (2023, May 03). How to Teach Sustainable Investing to Kids. Retrieved from https://classtechtips.com/2023/05/03/what-is-sustainable-invest ing/

ANSWER KEY

Chapter 1

Chapter 2

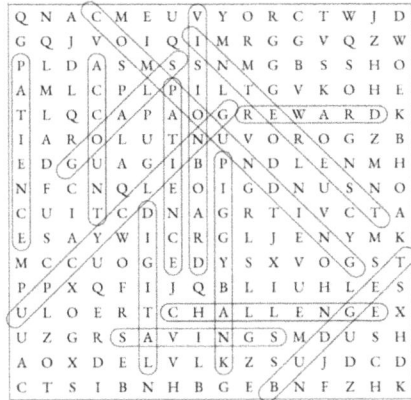

Chapter 3

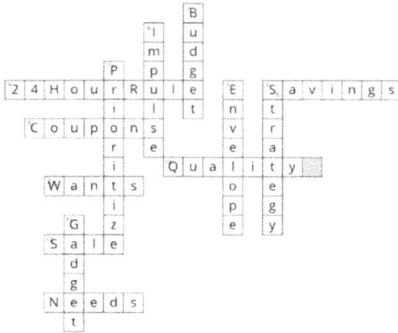

Chapter 6

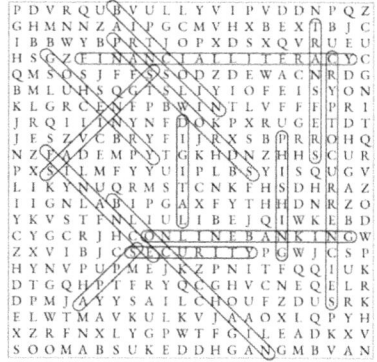

A STRESS-FREE GUIDE TO FINANCIAL LITERACY FOR TEENS & YOUNG ADULTS

MASTER MONEY MANAGEMENT, AVOID COSTLY MISTAKES, INVEST LIKE A PRO, AND SECURE YOUR FINANCIAL FUTURE

MONEY MENTOR PUBLICATIONS

TABLE OF CONTENTS

GET YOUR FREE
INTERACTIVE BUDGET TRACKING
SPREADSHEET

SCAN FOR
A FREE
TEMPLATE

EASILY TRACK INCOME AND EXPENSES FOR 9 DIFFERENT
CATEGORIES

MONEY MENTOR PUBLICATIONS

INTRODUCTION

Have you ever been hit with a sudden, "Wait, how am I supposed to do this?" feeling when trying to figure out how to manage your first paycheck, deciding whether to splurge on that new phone or save up for your first car? You're not alone. Most of us have stared at our bank statements in confusion, wishing we had a guide to decode all the financial mumbo jumbo. It feels like everyone else got a crash course in managing money while we're left scrambling to figure it out on our own. One of the most crucial lessons teens and young adults need is how to handle money wisely, yet our schools often leave us in the dark on this important subject.

That's exactly why this book exists. It's here to translate the complex language of finance into something you can understand and use. It's a guide from financial confusion to clarity and empowerment, written specifically for you, the teen or young adult stepping into the world of money management.

This isn't your typical finance book. We've tossed out the boring lectures and infused the pages with stories you'll actually want to read. Expect to see anecdotes that mirror your experiences and real-world examples that make sense. Why? Because learning about money doesn't have to be a snooze fest.

The goal here is simple: to make you financially literate in a world where digital banking, cryptocurrency, and the gig economy are becoming the norm. We're talking about real skills that will help you navigate your daily financial decisions and plan for a future where you're in charge.

Alarmingly, many teens and young adults are left out of the loop when it comes to financial education. Did you know that 75% of people your age feel clueless about managing their finances? This gap can lead to anxiety, unnecessary debt, and missed opportunities. It doesn't have to be this way.

You—the YouTube-watching, meme-sharing, TikTok-scrolling generation—are ready to change the narrative. You dream of financial independence, making smart investment choices, and avoiding the debt traps that snagged previous generations. This book is here to help you do just that.

We'll tackle everything from crafting a budget that fits your lifestyle to understanding how to start investing with just a little cash. We'll decode the mysteries of credit scores, explore ways to boost your earnings, and even dive into the basics of taxes.

We know what you might be thinking: "I don't have enough money to manage," or "Finance books are too dense." Hear us out. This book is crafted with your concerns in mind. It's tailored for beginners and packed with interactive tools that you can personalize. Most importantly, it's written in a style that speaks to you—not at you.

So, let's kick-start this journey together. By the end of this book, you will be equipped to make informed financial decisions and feel confident about securing a future where you call the financial shots. Ready to take control of your money? Let's get started.

CHAPTER 1

FINANCIAL FOUNDATIONS: BUILDING YOUR KNOWLEDGE FROM THE GROUND UP

The number one problem in today's generation and economy is the lack of financial literacy.

ALAN GREENSPAN

Getting ready to step out into the world on your own two feet for the first time is a rush—exciting, a bit scary, and undeniably liberating. It's like standing on the edge of a new world where every decision is yours, from what you eat for breakfast to how late you stay up. Among these newfound freedoms, one superpower stands above the rest: managing your money. Get this right, and you're in control; get it wrong, and you could be in for a turbulent ride that impacts your life for years to come. No pressure, right? Remember, knowledge is power! The more you know about how to handle your finances, the more freedom and security you will have in the future!

Let's discover what can happen when money management skills are neglected during your student years.

1.1 THE RISKS OF IGNORING FINANCIAL EDUCATION

1. Independence Delay - *Ethan's Epiphany*

During his senior year of high school, Ethan landed his first part-time job at a local café and relished the freedom that came with his first paycheck. Eager to enjoy his earnings, he splurged on a new gaming console and nights out with friends, overlooking his parents' advice to save. As graduation approached, Ethan dreamed of moving out and starting his independent life. However, when the time came to put down a deposit for an apartment, Ethan realized that he hadn't saved nearly enough to cover the initial expenses. Unable to afford the move, he had to delay his plans for independence and stay at home longer than he wanted, struggling to save up while watching his peers embark on their new lives. This frustrating setback taught Ethan the value of financial foresight and saving for major life steps.

2. Overwhelmed by Overdrafts - *Emily's Tale*

Emily was thrilled to start her college life and be independent. With her first bank account, she felt ready to handle her own finances. Excited by her new freedom, she splurged on dorm decorations, new clothes, and hanging out with friends. However, Emily didn't keep track of her spending. By the end of the first month, she faced multiple bank overdraft fees after exceeding her account balance. Each purchase pushed her deeper into the red, culminating in over $100 in bank fees. This harsh lesson taught Emily the importance of budgeting and monitoring her bank account regularly to avoid drowning in avoidable fees.

3. Credit Card Chaos - *Josh's Journey*

Josh received his first credit card with a $1,000 limit as he entered university. He viewed it as free money, using it to fund extravagant outings and electronics to enhance his college experience. Josh quickly maxed out his card without understanding the impact of high interest and minimum payments. When the bill arrived, he could only afford the minimum payment, not realizing that it barely covered the interest. This led to a ballooning balance and a plummeting credit score. It took Josh years to recover, learning the hard way that credit isn't an extension of income.

4. The Hidden Costs of Renting - *Lara's Lesson*

Lara signed her first apartment lease without reviewing the terms closely or understanding the full cost of living on her own. Excited to be independent, she overlooked expenses like utilities, internet, and renter's insurance, which were not included in the rent. Midway through the semester, Lara struggled to cover these additional costs, forcing her to skimp on essentials like food and heating. This experience taught her to review all lease and utility agreements meticulously and to plan a comprehensive budget that includes all living expenses, avoiding financial strains that can come from unexpected bills.

Stepping into independence doesn't have to mean stumbling through financial pitfalls. Arm yourself with the right know-how from this guide, and you're set to sail smoothly over the hurdles that trip up the unprepared. Dive into these pages, and you'll gather golden nuggets of wisdom that will have you managing your money like a boss. Picture a life where financial fumbles don't darken your days or burden your future. By adopting good money habits now, you'll dodge the stress and anxiety that plague many, basking in freedom and choice that others can only envy. Every smart save, wise spend, and insightful investment steers your present, secures your independence, and carves out a thriving future exactly as you envision it.

Imagine starting your own business or diving into the world of real estate with confidence. These aren't just dreams—they're entirely achievable realities with a solid financial foundation laid down early. Embrace these skills now, and not only will you easily navigate life's monetary challenges, but you'll also stand miles ahead of your peers. While they're still wrestling with the basics, you'll be mastering the art of making your money work for you.

1.2 UNLOCKING THE POWER OF FINANCIAL LITERACY

Financial literacy isn't just about numbers; it's about gaining control over your financial life. It means knowing how to budget so you don't end up broke before payday, saving so you have a cushion for emergencies, and investing wisely to grow your wealth. It's also about managing debt without getting buried and understanding how credit works so you don't get hit with high interest rates. Being financially literate helps you make smart choices with your money, like whether to splurge or to save for future goals. It's about reading financial statements without getting lost, grasping how interest rates can affect you, and keeping a good credit score. In short, it's about setting yourself up for financial stability, avoiding unnecessary debt, and building wealth over time.

Mellody Hobson, Chairperson of Starbucks, said it best:

If you understand how money can work for you and against you, you can make better decisions. Financial literacy is not about wealth but about understanding money regardless of the amount. It's about how you treat it and how you maximize opportunities.

Let's look at some examples of how learning good money skills now will help you get ahead of the curve.

1. Jameson's Smart Savings

Jameson, a high school senior, started saving a portion of his allowance and part-time job earnings early on. He opened a high-yield savings account and set up automatic transfers to ensure he consistently saved money. By the time he graduated, Jameson had saved enough to cover his first year of college expenses, reducing his reliance on student loans and giving him a financial head start.

2. Jenna's Budgeting Success

Jenna, a college freshman, created a budget as soon as she started receiving her scholarship funds and part-time job earnings. She used budgeting apps to track her spending, ensuring she lived within her means. By avoiding unnecessary expenses and prioritizing her needs, Jenna saved a significant amount of money each month, which she later used to study abroad without financial stress.

3. AJ's Investment Journey

AJ, a 19-year-old college student, took a personal finance course in high school that sparked his interest in investing. He started small by investing in low-cost index funds and learning about the stock market through books and online resources. By regularly contributing to his investment portfolio and taking advantage of compound interest, AJ saw steady growth in his investments, setting himself up for long-term financial success.

4. Korinne's Entrepreneurial Spirit

Korinne, a teenager passionate about baking, turned her hobby into a small business. She carefully managed her earnings, reinvesting in her business and saving a portion of her profits. By keeping track of her expenses and setting financial goals, Korinne expanded her business and saved enough to fund her college education without taking on debt.

Dedicating time to learning personal finance is one of the best investments you can make. It puts you in control of your future, reduces money-related stress, and opens doors to financial independence. The good news is that you don't need to make a lot of money to achieve financial independence; it's not about how much you earn but how you manage what you have. Many believe a high salary guarantees financial security, but that's not always the case. There are countless examples of millionaires who have worked blue-collar jobs their entire lives, diligently saving and investing wisely.

On the other hand, some doctors and other professionals earning substantial incomes find themselves broke due to poor financial habits and excessive spending. Financial independence hinges on living within your means, budgeting effectively, saving consistently, and making smart investments. By adopting these practices, you can build wealth and achieve financial stability regardless of income level. So, don't wait—start building your financial knowledge today and enjoy the benefits for years to come.

1.3 NAVIGATING YOUR BANK ACCOUNT: WHAT ALL THE TERMS MEAN

If you don't already have your own bank account, the time has come to get one. There are a lot of banks and credit unions to choose from, so here are a few things to consider when opening that first account:

Fees and Charges

- **Monthly Maintenance Fees**: Look for accounts with no or low monthly fees. Many banks offer free student checking accounts or accounts with fee waivers if certain conditions are met, such as maintaining a minimum balance or setting up direct deposit.
- **ATM Fees**: Consider the availability of ATMs and whether the bank charges fees for using out-of-network ATMs. Some banks offer reimbursements for these fees.
- **Overdraft Fees**: Check the bank's overdraft policy and associated fees. Some banks offer overdraft protection plans that link to a savings account to cover transactions.

Account Features

- **Interest Rates**: Compare the interest rates offered on savings accounts, checking accounts, and certificates of deposit (CDs). Higher interest rates can help your money grow faster.
- **Mobile and Online Banking**: Ensure the bank provides robust online and mobile banking services. Features to look for include mobile check deposit, bill pay, and account alerts.
- **Minimum Balance Requirements**: Some accounts require a minimum balance to avoid fees or to earn interest. Make sure these requirements align with your financial situation.

Accessibility and Convenience

- **Branch Locations**: If you prefer in-person banking services, consider the convenience of branch locations.

Some online banks have limited or no physical branches but may offer other benefits.

- **Customer Service**: Research the bank's reputation for customer service. Look for reviews and ratings to see how current customers feel about their experiences.
- **Ease of Account Opening**: Check the process for opening an account. Some banks offer entirely online account opening processes, which can be more convenient.

Security and Trust

- **FDIC/NCUA Insurance**: Ensure the bank or credit union is insured by the FDIC (Federal Deposit Insurance Corporation) or the NCUA (National Credit Union Administration). This insurance protects your deposits up to $250,000.
- **Security Features**: Look for security features, such as two-factor authentication, fraud alerts, and secure login processes, to protect your account information.

Credit Union vs. Bank

- **Credit Unions**: These often offer lower fees and better interest rates on loans and savings accounts because they are non-profit institutions owned by their members. However, membership may be restricted to certain groups.
- **Banks**: These typically offer more products and services, including a wider range of loans, credit cards, and investment services. They also tend to have more branch locations and ATMs.

Special Programs and Benefits

- **Student Accounts**: Many banks offer special accounts designed for students, which may include perks, such as waived fees or discounts on loans.
- **Rewards Programs**: Some banks offer rewards programs for using their debit or credit cards, which can provide cash back, points, or other incentives.

If you already have your account, let's be honest: the first time you opened it, it may have felt a bit like venturing into a bizarre new universe where everything seemed overly complicated. You were probably handed a stack of paperwork thicker than your favorite diner's menu, with a lot of unfamiliar terms and options. Well, it's time to sort all that out. From checking accounts that feel like your financial "checking in" points to savings accounts that are more like your money's cozy long-term home, understanding these can make you feel less like you're reading a foreign language and more like you're taking charge of your cash.

Account Types: More Than Just Places to Stash Your Cash

First are *Checking Accounts*. These are your everyday financial toolboxes. They're perfect for daily transactions, like getting that burrito from the food truck or paying your electric bill. They usually come with a debit card, which might become your new best friend for easy access to your funds. While they're convenient for frequent use, they're not meant to grow your wealth.

Switch gears to *Savings Accounts*, and you're entering a different vibe. Here's where your money sits back, relaxes, and slowly grows through something magical called interest, the money the bank pays you to keep your money there. It's similar to planting and watching a tree grow over the years. You won't use a savings account for daily expenses; rather, it's perfect for your long-term goals, like that summer road trip, your own car, or perhaps eventually, a down payment on your first condo.

There are also hybrids and specialties: ***Money Market Accounts*** and ***Certificates of Deposit (CDs)***. Money market accounts are like the cool cousins of the regular savings account, typically offering higher interest rates in return for higher balance requirements. CDs? Think of them as time capsules for your cash. You lock away your money at a fixed interest rate for a set period, and—Bam!—more money at the end of the term.

Understanding Fees: Dodge Those Sneaky Charges

Now, on to something less fun—bank fees. Have you ever been slapped with a fee for withdrawing your own money from an ATM that wasn't affiliated with your bank? Maybe you've felt the sting of an overdraft fee when you miscalculated and spent more than what was in your account. These fees sneak up on you, but there are ways to outsmart them. For ATMs, it's about knowing where your bank's machines are located or getting an account that offers ATM fee rebates. Overdraft fees? Opt into alerts that notify you when you're close to zero or link your checking to your savings for automatic coverage. You can discuss available options when you open your bank account, or if it's already up and running, visit your bank and ask them about all of the features they have to help you avoid unnecessary fees. Your goal is never to pay a dime in bank fees, and it is 100% possible with a little care and attention.

Banking Services: Your Financial Swiss Army Knife

Today's online banking features are all about convenience and efficiency. Most banks now offer features like automatic transfers, which you can set up to funnel money into your savings account or to pay bills automatically. It's like setting a cruise control for your financial obligations; once you set it, you can sit back and focus on other things.

Alerts are another game changer. Get a text or email when your balance dips below a certain amount or when a large transaction goes through. Since you'll be the first to know if something's up with your accounts, you have peace of mind. Many banks also offer spending insights, showing you pie charts or bar graphs of your monthly spending divided into categories. It's a quick and visual way to get a sense of where your money is going without digging through all your statements.

Safety and Security: Protecting Your Treasure

Finally, let's talk about safety. In an age when data breaches seem as common as the latest TikTok that just went viral, knowing how to protect your bank account is crucial. First rule? Create strong, unique passwords for your online banking accounts. Think less "123456" and more "$ecureP@ssw0rd!2025." Also, always log out completely after accessing banking info on public or shared computers. Your bank plays defense with measures like encryption and fraud monitoring. However, staying informed about the latest security, like two-factor authentication, adds an extra layer of armor around your finances.

We started this chapter by highlighting the significance of financial literacy in establishing a solid foundation for managing personal finances and avoiding common pitfalls. Next, we'll dive into the intricacies of budgeting, but before that, here's a handy checklist to guide you through setting up your bank account effectively:

ACTION STEPS FOR SETTING UP YOUR BANK ACCOUNT:

1. Research Banks and Credit Unions:

- Compare fees and charges.
- Evaluate account features like interest rates and mobile banking.
- Consider accessibility and convenience.

2. Understand Account Types:

- Know the differences among checking, savings, money market accounts, and CDs.

3. Review Fees:

- Look for accounts with no or low monthly maintenance fees.
- Be aware of ATM and overdraft fees, and explore options for overdraft protection.

4. Examine Account Features:

- Be sure that there are robust online and mobile banking services.
- Verify minimum balance requirements and other requirements.

5. Evaluate Security:

- Ensure that the bank is insured by FDIC or NCUA.
- Look for strong security features like two-factor authentication.

6. Explore Special Programs:

- Investigate student accounts and rewards programs.

CHAPTER 2
BUDGETING BASICS

A Budget is telling your money where to go instead of wondering where it went.

DAVE RAMSEY

I magine you're at your favorite restaurant with friends, menu in hand. Do you splurge on that overpriced but oh-so-tempting gourmet entrée, or do you stick with the more budget-friendly option? Life is full of these little choices when what you decide in the moment can impact your wallet in bigger ways than you might think. That's where a solid budget comes into play—not as a buzzkill to all your fun, but as a financial GPS guiding you through daily decisions and beyond. Let's break down the art of budgeting.

2.1 CRAFTING YOUR FIRST BUDGET: A STEP-BY-STEP GUIDE

Setting Financial Goals: A Compass for Your Cash

Setting financial goals is like picking a destination before you start driving; it's essential. Without a destination, you might go in circles or, even worse, get lost in the middle of nowhere. Financial goals work the same way. They give your money a purpose and keep you motivated, whether it's saving up for a concert ticket, managing car payments, or making your first investments.

Start by distinguishing between short-term and long-term goals. Short-term goals might include saving for a new laptop or funding a weekend road trip. These are typically goals you can achieve within a year. Long-term goals require more time and commitment, like saving for a car or education. Both types of goals are important; they just play different roles in your financial strategy. By identifying these, you're creating a blueprint that aligns your financial habits with your personal aspirations, making each dollar work toward something meaningful.

Tracking Income and Expenses: Your Financial Mirror

Now, let's get into the nitty-gritty—tracking your income and expenses. You need a clear picture of what comes in and what goes out. Start by listing all your sources of income, including that part-time job and any side hustles. Then, dive into your expenses. This means all of them—rent, food, subscriptions, gas/bus money—each penny needs to be accounted for.

This might sound tedious, and you might be tempted to estimate, but resist the urge. Estimations can lead to financial blind spots. Use tools like banking apps, spreadsheets, or even good old pen and paper to keep track. The good news is that you don't have to reinvent the wheel when it comes to finding a free downloadable interactive budget spreadsheet that will work for you. A simple Google search for "Free Google Sheets budget template" or "Free Excel budget templates" will give you many options to choose from.

You can also download our free budget tracking spreadsheet here: https://bit.ly/3yXeT0w

The most important thing is to take action and do it! It will help you understand your spending behaviors so you can adjust them to align with your financial goals.

In an effort to keep it real, we need to let you know that life is more expensive than you think it will be. Inflation over the last few years is giving everyone a bit of sticker shock when it comes to buying the essentials.

If you are still living at home, your budget will look different from someone who is already living on their own. Here's a list of potential expenses you need to prepare for as you move on to the next phase of your life:

Upfront Costs

- **Security Deposit**: Typically, landlords require one to two months' rent to cover potential damages. You may be able to get some or all of this back when you move out.
- **First and Last Month's Rent**: Many landlords require both upfront.
- **Application Fees**: There may also be costs for background and credit checks.

- **Moving Costs**: You may need to rent a moving truck and/or buy packing supplies.
- **Utility Deposits**: Deposits are used to set up services like electricity, gas, water, and internet.

Recurring Monthly Expenses

- **Rent**: The primary expense varies widely by location.
- **Utilities**: Read your lease carefully to see what is and isn't included, such as electricity, gas, water, sewer, and trash removal.
- **Internet and Cable**: This includes connectivity, data, and entertainment costs.
- **Renter's Insurance**: This provides coverage for personal belongings and liability.
- **Groceries**: Obviously, this includes food and household supplies.
- **Transportation**: You may have car payments, insurance, gas, and vehicle maintenance, or you may have public transportation costs.

Household Essentials

- **Furniture**: Bed, couch, tables, chairs, and other essential furniture
- **Kitchen Supplies**: Pots, pans, utensils, dishes, and small appliances
- **Cleaning Supplies**: Vacuum, mop, cleaning products, and other essentials
- **Bathroom Supplies**: Towels, shower curtains, toiletries, and cleaning items
- **Bedding**: Sheets, pillows, blankets, and mattress protectors

Additional Expenses

- **Laundry**: Costs for in-unit laundry or using laundromats
- **Personal Care Items**: Shampoo, soap, toothpaste, and other personal hygiene products
- **Entertainment and Dining Out**: Budgeted costs for social activities and eating out
- **Health Insurance**: Premiums if not covered under a parent's plan or provided by your employer
- **Emergency Fund**: Savings for unexpected expenses like medical emergencies or car repairs
- **Subscription Services**: Streaming services, magazines, gym memberships, etc.

Miscellaneous

- **Repairs and Maintenance**: Minor repairs and maintenance not covered by the landlord
- **Decor**: Items to personalize your space, like artwork, plants, and rugs
- **Storage**: Costs for renting additional storage space if needed

Remember to plan for all the little things you've never had to think about before, like toilet tissue, dishwashing detergent, and garbage bags. They add up quickly and can affect your overall budget.

Allocating Funds: Divide and Conquer

With a clear understanding of your income and expenses, it's time to allocate your funds. Think of your money as a pie you can slice in various ways. Some slices might be bigger, like rent or tuition, while others might be smaller, like entertainment or dining out. Here's the trick: prioritize your essentials first—housing, food, transportation, and necessary bills. The slice that's left can be divided among your savings and a few extras that you want.

A practical approach here is the 50/30/20 rule, in which 50% of your income goes to needs, 30% to wants, and 20% to savings. Adjust these percentages based on what best fits your situation. Maybe you're in a tight spot, and it will be more like 70/20/10. It's okay. The goal is to create a balance that supports stability but still allows room for enjoyment.

Adjusting Your Budget: Staying Agile

Your first budget won't be perfect. It's a living document that evolves. Regular check-ins are key. Sit down at least monthly to review how well your budget works. Are you consistently over-spending in one area? Do you have a little more wiggle room than expected? Adjustments might be necessary, and that's perfectly fine.

Life throws curveballs—unexpected expenses like a phone screen repair or a traffic ticket. Your budget needs to be flexible enough to accommodate these without derailing your financial goals.

Budget Adjustment Checklist

To help you stay on top of your budget adjustments, here's a handy checklist:

1. **Review your financial goals:** Are they still relevant? Have your priorities shifted?
2. **Analyze your spending:** Look for patterns or areas where you consistently overspend.
3. **Adjust your allocations:** Modify your budget slices to better fit your current needs.

4. **Plan for surprises:** Always have a small buffer for unexpected expenses.

Regular use of this checklist can turn a once-daunting task into a quick and simple routine, ensuring your budget remains an effective tool for financial success.

Saving vs. Splurging: Balancing Act of the Century

Here's the million-dollar question: how do you decide when to save and when to splurge? Imagine you're a chef creating a dish, trying to balance flavors perfectly. Just as you carefully measure each ingredient to create harmony, you'll want to find the right balance in your finances, too.

Start with understanding the value of what you're buying. Does it add to your life in a meaningful way, or is it just going to collect dust?

An easy trick is to calculate the cost per use. For instance, that expensive pair of boots might seem like a splurge, but if you wear them every day this winter, the cost per wear makes them a bargain compared to a cheap pair that falls apart after a few uses.

Another approach is to calculate how many hours you will have to work to pay for a particular thing, which also gives you some perspective and helps you to decide if it is really worth it.

Another tactic is to set waiting periods for large purchases. Give yourself a set time, maybe a week or two, before pulling the trigger on anything that costs more than a set amount. This cooling-off period can save you from impulse buys you might regret later. If you still want it just as much after the wait, and if it fits within your budget without derailing your savings goals, it's likely a worthwhile purchase.

Avoid overspending. Recognizing your triggers to overspend is like tuning into your personal frequency. Start by identifying what prompts you to reach for your wallet. Is it a stressful shift at work, a scroll through social media, or perhaps an "on-sale" sign that you can't resist? Once you know your triggers, you can set up guardrails. For example, avoid browsing online stores when you're bored or stressed. Instead, distract yourself with a hobby or chat with a friend.

Making a game out of frugal living can be both fun and rewarding. Challenge yourself to find treasures at garage sales, thrift stores, and bargain bins. You'd be amazed at what people are willing to part with for a fraction of the original price. Repurposing items is another creative way to save. Turn an old ladder into a bookshelf, or use mason jars as stylish storage. The thrill of the hunt and the satisfaction of a good deal can make thrifty living feel like an exciting adventure rather than a chore.

2.2 THE IMPACT OF SOCIAL MEDIA ON SPENDING HABITS

Social media significantly impacts the buying habits of teens and young adults by creating a constant stream of targeted advertisements and influencer endorsements that can be hard to resist. Platforms like Instagram, TikTok, and Snapchat are designed to keep users engaged, often showcasing trendy products and lifestyle images that promote a desire by users to emulate what they see. The ease of in-app shopping and the instant gratification of making a purchase with just a few clicks further fuel impulsive buying. Additionally, social media often blurs the line between genuine recommendations and paid promotions, making it challenging for users to distinguish between them. This constant exposure can lead to increased spending, often on non-essential items, and can contribute to financial strain and the development of poor money management habits.

The mechanics of this influence go beyond direct advertising. These platforms can also exacerbate social comparison, the insidious thief of joy. Seeing peers and influencers living what appears to be a higher standard of life can spark an internal desire to match or exceed that standard. You might find yourself splurging on brands tagged by influencers, booking a vacation to the "Insta-famous" beach you've seen all over your feed, or hunting down the dining set that perfectly matches the one in that viral Pinterest post. Social media platforms are designed to be addictive—the more time you spend on them, the more opportunities they have to learn what makes you tick and then tailor ads that tap directly into your desires.

Building Digital Resilience: Crafting Your Shield Against Consumerist Culture

It's possible to conquer the urge to impulse buy on social media by implementing a few mindful strategies. Start by pruning out influencers and brands that trigger your spending impulses or make you feel inadequate. Replace them with content that enriches your life and aligns with your values, like pages focused on budget travel, DIY home decor, or thrift fashion. This doesn't mean you can't follow any luxury brands or influencers, but it helps create a balance that keeps you grounded rather than always reaching for your wallet.

Additionally, become a savvy observer. Start recognizing targeted ads —those sneaky sales pitches that pop up after you've just searched for a product or talked about it near your smartphone. Most social media platforms offer options to control the ads you see, so take advantage of those settings to reduce the onslaught of temptation. It's also helpful to remind yourself that what you're seeing is often a highlight reel, not everyday reality. Those perfect moments captured on Instagram are just that—moments. They don't represent the full picture of anyone's life, including the debts or sacrifices made for that snapshot-worthy scene.

FOMO and Managing It: Turning Fear into Freedom

FOMO, or the Fear of Missing Out, is the pulse that often drives social media's influence on spending. It's the fear that everyone else is having a better time, owning better things, or living a better life—and it can lead to impulsive spending as you try to buy your way into the club of perceived happiness. Combatting FOMO starts with turning inward. Reflect on what truly brings you joy and satisfaction beyond the fleeting thrill of a purchase. Is it spending time with loved ones, pursuing a hobby, or maybe just the peace that comes with having no debt?

When you feel the tug of FOMO, pause and assess your motives. Are you considering a purchase because it genuinely aligns with your goals, or are you trying to fill a void that social media has magnified? Sometimes, the best way to manage FOMO is to log off and engage in real-life activities that reinforce your values and boost your mood. Engage in sports, go for a hike, visit a museum, or cook a new recipe. These activities distract from social media-induced desires and build a life that feels fulfilling offline.

Creating a Positive Online Environment: Your Financial Wellness Zone

Turning your social media environment into a positive space starts with intentionality. Follow financial educators, minimalism advocates, and personal development coaches, who often share content that can inspire you to make thoughtful spending decisions. Many of these accounts provide tips on financial planning, smart investing, and reducing waste, which can help shift your perspective from spending to saving and investing in your future.

Reflection Exercise - Social Media and Spending

- List the last five non-essential items you purchased and what inspired those purchases. How many were influenced by social media?

_____

_____

_____

- Reflect on how these purchases have contributed to your life. Do they bring you lasting happiness or satisfaction?

_____

_____

_____

- How can you change your social media feeds to support your financial goals and reduce impulsive spending?

_____

_____

_____

By engaging in such reflections, you can draw boundaries that protect your financial health from the persuasive power of social media. Remember that every dollar you don't spend on fleeting trends is a dollar you can invest in your future—whether through savings, investments, or spending on experiences that have lasting meaning in your life.

2.3 APPS AND TOOLS TO SIMPLIFY BUDGETING

If you are like us, the idea of sitting down with a stack of receipts and a calculator to manage your finances is about as appealing as watching paint dry. What if you could turn that chore into something as easy and engaging as scrolling through your social media feed? Enter the world of budgeting apps and financial tools, your new best friends in the saga of money management. These aren't just bland, number-crunching robots; they're designed to fit seamlessly into your lifestyle, offering both simplicity and a dash of fun.

Budgeting Apps: Your Financial Dashboard

Wouldn't it be nice to have a personal finance advisor who is always ready to tell you how much you can spend on those new shoes or whether you need to tighten the belt this week? That's essentially what a budgeting app does. There are several budgeting apps to choose from, so go ahead and search for those devoted YouTubers who have already done the homework for you by outlining the pros and cons of each one. Here are just a few of the options to consider: *Monarch*, *NerdWallet*, *Rocket Money*, *EveryDollar*, *YNAB* (You Need a Budget), *Quicken Simplifi*, and *PocketGuard*. Some are free to use, while others require a subscription to access more advanced features. Taking a bit of time upfront to find the best fit for you and your lifestyle is definitely worth it. It can be life-changing when you can easily make a budget and track your expenses with the touch of a button.

Custom Tools: Tailor-Made Budgeting Solutions

While apps and software are great, sometimes you need something tailor-made for your unique financial situation. That's where tools like spreadsheets come in. Google Sheets or Microsoft Excel can become powerful allies in managing your finances. You can create custom categories, formulas to calculate savings goals, and charts to visualize your progress. It's a bit more DIY, but it allows for complete customization.

Spreadsheets are especially great for those who love diving into the details. You can track fluctuations in your spending, calculate how changes in one area affect your overall budget, and experiment with different saving scenarios to see how they impact your goals. It's a more hands-on approach, but it's a perfect fit for the data nerds among us.

In short, managing your money has never been easier or more accessible. Whether you're a fan of sleek apps that do most of the work for you, comprehensive software that provides deep dives into financial planning, or custom tools that let you tweak every detail, there's something out there that fits your lifestyle. These tools simplify the process and make it more engaging, turning the daunting task of budgeting into a manageable and even enjoyable part of your daily routine. Explore what these tools have to offer, and take control of your financial future with confidence.

2.4 AVOIDING COMMON BUDGETING PITFALLS FOR TEENS AND YOUNG ADULTS

Let's face it, we'd all like budgeting to be simply lining up numbers and patting ourselves on the back for staying under budget. However, sometimes it's more like walking through a minefield where small missteps can blow our financial plans to smithereens. It's easy to slip up, especially when you're a teen or young adult balancing classes, maybe a job, and that all-important social life. Recognizing these pitfalls is the first step in dodging them. With a little foresight, you can sidestep these budget busters like a pro.

Overlooking Small Expenses: The Silent Budget Killers

Ever find yourself wondering where all your money went, even though you've been avoiding big purchases? Those small, almost invisible expenses are likely the culprits. A soft drink here, an app purchase there, a snack from the vending machine—individually, they seem inconsequential, but together, they can gnaw away at your wallet like nothing else.

The key to keeping these little spendthrifts in check is awareness. Start by tracking every penny you spend—yes, even the $2.50 on a soft drink. Use a spending tracker app or even a simple spreadsheet. This might sound monotonous, but seeing a month's worth of nickels and dimes laid out is eye-opening. Once you identify the patterns, set specific limits for these small expenses. Maybe allocate a "fun money" budget that allows for these little pleasures without letting them overrun your financial goals. It's all about balance – allowing yourself those small indulgences without letting them derail your budget.

Failing to Plan for Irregular Expenses: The Budgeting Blind Spots

Then there are those irregular expenses that don't come around every month but hit hard when they do—think about things like regular car maintenance and registration, annual subscriptions, or birthday and Christmas gifts for friends and family. These aren't surprises; they're certainties with irregular timing. Failing to plan for these can throw your budget into chaos, forcing you to dip into savings or, worse, rack up credit card debt.

To combat this, make a list of annual or semi-annual expenses you can predict. Divide the total cost by 12, and tuck away that amount each month into a dedicated savings account. This way, when the expense is due, you've got the funds ready and waiting. Knowing you'll need a new pair of sneakers for the upcoming track season and setting aside a little each month allows you to stride into the store and pick the pair you really want without sweating the price tag.

Expense	Annual Cost ($)	Monthly Savings ($)
Car Insurance	1200	100
Car Registration	240	20
Holiday Gifts	600	50
Track Sneakers	120	10
Annual Subscriptions	60	5
Savings Needed Per Month		**$185**

Neglecting Savings: The Non-negotiable Financial Pillar

Lastly, let's talk about savings. Often seen as the leftover piece of the budget pie, savings should actually be one of the first slices you cut. Neglecting to save is like skipping the foundations when building a house. Sure, you might put up the structure faster, but how long before cracks appear?

Treat savings as a **non-negotiable expense**. Decide on a percentage of your income to save each month, and stick to it as if it were a bill that must be paid. Automate your savings if you can. Set up your bank account to transfer the funds to a savings account every payday. Automation makes savings invisible and painless. It's not about how much you save initially but about developing the habit. Over time, as your income grows, you can increase the amount, building a robust financial cushion that will serve you well in emergencies and help fund larger future goals. Another savings hack for the tech-savvy is to leverage apps like *Acorns*, *Chime*, and *Greenlight* (great for kids & teens) that round up your change from everyday purchases and save the difference. You'd be surprised by how quickly those pennies can add up.

In wrapping up this chapter, let's circle back to the essence of effective budgeting for teens and young adults like you. It's not about restriction; it's about making informed choices that align with your values and goals. By being mindful of the pitfalls – those sneaky small expenses, the irregular but inevitable costs, the allure of impulse buys, and the critical role of savings, you set the stage for a financial strategy that supports not just your current needs, but also your long-term aspirations. As we transition into the next chapter, keep these insights in mind. They are the building blocks for the more advanced financial planning and decision-making we'll explore next, where we dive deeper into maximizing your financial potential through smart saving, investing and income strategies. Stay tuned, and remember that every step you take now is a step toward a financially secure and fulfilling future.

ACTION STEPS FOR BUDGETING BASICS

1. Craft Your First Budget

Set Financial Goals

- Define short-term goals (e.g., saving for a new laptop).
- Define long-term goals (e.g., saving for a car or education).

Track Income and Expenses

- List all sources of income (part-time job, freelance gigs, etc.).
- List all expenses (rent, food, subscriptions, transportation, etc.).
- Use tools like banking apps, spreadsheets, or pen and paper for accuracy.

Allocate Funds

- Prioritize essential expenses (housing, food, transportation).
- Use the 50/30/20 rule, adjusting percentages based on your needs.

2. Plan for Irregular Expenses

Identify annual or semi-annual expenses (car maintenance, subscriptions, gifts, etc.).

- Calculate the total cost and divide by 12 to determine how much to save monthly.
- Set up a dedicated savings account for these expenses.

3. Save Consistently

Treat savings as a non-negotiable expense.

- Decide on a percentage of your income to save each month.
- Automate your savings.

4. Adjust Your Budget Regularly

Review your budget monthly.

- Analyze spending patterns and adjust allocations as needed.
- Plan for unexpected expenses, and maintain a buffer.

5. Manage Small and Impulse Expenses

Track all small expenses to identify patterns.

- Set specific limits for non-essential spending.
- Use waiting periods for large purchases to avoid impulsive buys.

CHAPTER 3
MASTERING MONEY SAVING TECHNIQUES

If you want to get rich, think of saving as earning.

ANDREW CARNEGIE

Picture this: You're browsing through the latest sneaker drops online, and there's this one pair that's practically calling your name. Unfortunately, your wallet is on a strict budget of instant noodles and dreams. Before you give up and resign yourself to wearing your old, worn-out kicks, let's discuss some smart strategies to boost your savings on a low income. Learn how to make your money work harder so you can indulge in your interests without constantly feeling the pinch.

3.1 SMART SAVING STRATEGIES ON A SHOESTRING BUDGET

Saving money can sometimes feel like trying to fill a leaking bucket. You know it's smart to stash some cash for later, but the temptation to spend now can be overwhelming, especially when you're operating on a shoestring budget. Here's the scoop: saving isn't just about piling up cash for some distant, unknown future. It's about securing your peace of mind today and ensuring that you can handle whatever life throws at you tomorrow. So, how do you balance saving with living a life you enjoy now? Let's examine some strategies that can help without making you live on instant noodles (unless you're into that)

Prioritizing Savings: Why Your Future Self Will Thank You

Imagine your savings as a safety net or a launchpad; it's there to catch you if you fall and to propel you to new heights when you're ready to leap. Prioritizing savings means paying your future self first. It's tempting to think, "I'll save whatever's left at the end of the month." But let's be honest: how often is there anything left? Flipping the script means that you decide how much to save right off the bat when you plan your monthly budget, and then you adapt your spending to what remains.

To make this a habit, start small. Even a tiny amount, like 5% of your monthly income, is a solid start. The key is consistency. As your income increases, boost your savings rate proportionally. If you snag a raise or a better-paying gig, resist the urge to inflate your lifestyle in tandem. Keep your living standards steady, and funnel that extra cash into your savings. Before you know it, you'll have a tidy sum, and your future self? They're already throwing you a thank-you party.

Making Money Work for You: The Magic of Compound Interest

Now, let's talk about turning your savings into more savings without lifting a finger. Enter compound interest, which is basically your money making more money from the money it already made—yes, it's as great as it sounds. Here's the rundown: you earn interest not just on your initial savings but also on the interest that those savings earn. Over time, this snowballs, and your savings grow exponentially without additional work from you.

Here is a chart showing the magic of compounding interest over a 5-year period. Starting with a principal amount of $1,000 and an annual interest rate of 5%, you can see how the amount grows each year:

Year	Amount ($)
1	$ 1,050.00
2	$ 1,102.50
3	$ 1,157.63
4	$ 1,215.51
5	$ 1,276.28

To truly harness the power of compound interest, look for a savings account with a competitive interest rate, and let time do its thing. The key here is patience. Compound interest is a slow cooker, not a microwave, but the results are worth the wait.

Finding Extra Money to Save: Leave No Stones Unturned

Think you've tightened your belt to the last notch? Let's dig a bit deeper. There are generally overlooked money leaks in most budgets. Start by auditing your subscriptions—do you need that additional streaming plan, for instance? Next, evaluate your recurring purchases. Maybe you can swap branded products for generics, or cut down on those energy drinks. Each small saving adds up, providing more ammo for your savings arsenal. Use apps or websites to compare prices before making significant purchases to ensure that you're getting the best deal. Get inspired by frugal living gurus on YouTube and Instagram who are willing to share all of their money-saving secrets. Find one who is in your stage of life to get the most pertinent advice. Make saving money a game. It can be thrilling to find something you use regularly for a cheaper price.

Utilizing Cashback and Rewards Programs: Get Paid to Spend

If you have to spend money, you might as well get some of it back, right? Cashback and rewards programs can be the added bonus you didn't know existed. Whether it's a credit card that gives you cash back on purchases or a loyalty program at your favorite retailer, these programs can help you recover some cash from your spending. Just be sure to pay off credit balances in full each month to avoid interest charges that could eat up your cashback rewards.

Bulk Buying and Couponing: Old School but Gold

Here's where we get a bit old-school, but trust us, Grandma was on to something. Bulk buying and couponing can significantly slash your grocery bills. Buy non-perishables in bulk when they're on sale, and hunt down digital coupons for items you regularly use. Combine coupons with store sales for genius-level savings.

Minimizing Dining Out: Home Is Where the Savings Are

Eating out is fun, but cooking at home is the secret sauce to saving dough. Home-cooked meals are generally cheaper per serving compared to restaurant meals. Start with simple recipes and batch cooking. When it comes to food, plan your meals, shop with a list, and resist those expensive snack urges. The internet is swarming with free meal plans designed for people on a budget. The practice of cooking one meal and freezing leftovers for lunches or future dinners is a lot cheaper than cooking something different every day or eating out regularly. Also, turn cooking into a social event by hosting potluck dinners with friends instead of going out. You'll save money, improve your culinary skills, and maybe impress someone special with your newfound chef prowess.

Savings Challenges: Make Saving a Sport

Inject some fun into your savings routine with challenges. Try a no-spend month on non-essentials, or set a challenge to save a certain amount in a specified period. Make it a competition with friends to see who can save the most. These challenges can turn the mundane task of saving money into a more exciting endeavor.

Celebrating Milestones

Speaking of milestones, don't forget to celebrate them! Set up mini-rewards for when you hit certain savings targets. Maybe treat yourself to a nice meal out when you've saved your first $1000 towards your car fund, or buy that pair of shoes when you success-fully stick to your budget for three months straight. These celebra-tions act as positive reinforcement, making the act of saving feel more rewarding. Go ahead and give yourself a pat on the back to recognize the discipline it took to get there. By celebrating these wins, you reinforce the good behavior of saving and keep the moti-vation burning to reach the next milestone. After all, what's the fun in working toward a goal if you can't enjoy the journey along the way?

Reflection Section

Take a moment to reflect on which of these savings hacks you're excited to try first. Jot down a quick plan on how you'll implement it over the next month. Setting a clear, achievable goal can significantly increase the likelihood of sticking to your new savings strategy. Remember, each small step is a leap towards your financial independence.

_____

_____

_____

3.2 HIGH-YIELD SAVINGS ACCOUNTS: WHAT YOU NEED TO KNOW

Alright, so imagine you've been nurturing your savings in a regular account, and it's growing, sure, but it's kind of like watching paint dry. Slow and steady. Now, picture this: what if your savings could do a bit of heavy lifting on their own, bulking up like they've been hitting the gym hard? That's where high-yield savings accounts come into play, giving your money a chance to grow faster, without you having to lift a finger.

What Are High-Yield Savings Accounts

High-yield savings accounts are like the superheroes of the banking world. Unlike their mild-mannered cousin, the traditional savings account, these accounts offer a higher interest rate. Think of it as the difference between stashing your cash under a mattress versus investing in a venture that actually pays off. While the typical savings account might offer a meager 0.01% APY (Annual Percentage Yield), a high-yield account can soar to rates around 0.50% APY or more, depending on the market. This means that for every $1,000 you save, instead of earning just 10 cents in a year, you could earn $5 or more. Not exactly a fortune, but it's free money, and it's working on your behalf.

Benefits and Drawbacks

Now, sifting through the perks, the most glaringly obvious is that higher interest rate. It's passive income that accumulates faster than traditional savings, helping you reach financial goals more swiftly. Additionally, high-yield accounts often come with the same benefits as traditional savings accounts, like online access, transfer options, and sometimes, mobile check deposits. They make saving not just fruitful but also convenient.

However, no hero is without a flaw. High-yield accounts can come with strings attached. Some banks might require a higher minimum balance to maintain the account, or they might limit the number of free withdrawals you can make each month. And while the interest rates are attractive, they're often variable, subject to change based on the ebb and flow of the market. That means the impressive rate you sign up for might deflate a bit if the overall economic tide goes out.

Choosing the Right Account

When you're ready to pick a high-yield savings account, don't just jump at the first one with the highest interest rate. Look under the hood; check for any monthly maintenance fees or minimum balance requirements that could nibble away at your interest earnings. Also, consider the bank's reputation and customer service. You want a bank that's stable and makes you feel like a valued customer, not just an account number.

Online banks often offer higher rates than traditional brick-and-mortar banks because they have lower overhead costs. Don't shy away from them, but do your homework to ensure they're reputable. Check user reviews, and see what other customers have to say about their reliability and service. Remember, the goal is to make your savings work harder, not to add stress to your life.

Safety and Security

One common concern about stashing your cash in any bank account, but especially in an online one, is safety. Here's the good news: most high-yield savings accounts are offered by banks insured by the Federal Deposit Insurance Corporation (FDIC), which means your money is protected up to $250,000. If you're looking at credit unions, look for accounts insured by the National Credit Union Administration (NCUA). This insurance means that even if the bank fails, your money is safe.

In summary, high-yield savings accounts can be a potent tool in your financial arsenal. They offer higher interest rates, allowing your savings to grow faster and work harder. However, they're not free from drawbacks, such as potential minimum balance requirements and fluctuating interest rates. Choosing the right account demands a balance of favorable terms and robust security. Always ensure the institution is FDIC or NCUA insured, safeguarding your hard-earned cash.

As we wrap up this exploration of high-yield savings accounts, remember they are just one piece of the complex puzzle of personal finance. They're a fantastic tool for growing your savings, but they work best when used in conjunction with other smart financial strategies like budgeting, investing, and managing debt. In the next chapter, we delve deeper into the world of credit and debt management—a crucial arena for anyone looking to build a solid financial foundation. Stay tuned to learn how to navigate these waters safely and effectively, ensuring your financial journey is not just about saving but also about thriving.

3.3 ESTABLISHING YOUR EMERGENCY FUND: HOW MUCH IS ENOUGH?

Imagine this: you wake up to find your laptop, which is practically an extension of your own limbs, has decided to play dead. No amount of coaxing or cursing brings it back to life, and just like that, you're staring down the barrel of an unexpected—and pricey—laptop replacement. That's where an emergency fund steps in, your financial superhero, ready to swoop in and save the day. This isn't just about safeguarding against tech tragedies; it's about ensuring you're covered for any of life's unpredictable expenses, from medical bills to sudden job losses.

Importance of an Emergency Fund: Your Financial Safety Net

Think of an emergency fund as your financial safety net, cushioning you from the hard falls caused by life's surprises. Without it, every unexpected expense is a potential financial disaster that could send you spiraling into debt. The peace of mind that comes from knowing you have a stash of cash reserved exclusively for emergencies is priceless. It means you're not stressing over every little hiccup because you have a backup plan. It's like knowing there's a spare tire in your trunk —it might not be exciting, but if a tire blows, you'll be patting yourself on the back instead of pulling out your hair.

Calculating Your Needs: Tailoring Your Emergency Fund

So, how much do you actually need in this fund? The one-size-fits-all answer would be handy, but your emergency fund should reflect your personal circumstances. A good rule of thumb is to aim for three to six months' worth of living expenses. This range gives you a buffer substantial enough to handle most of what life could throw your way without leaving your finances in shambles.

Start by detailing your monthly necessities—rent, food, utilities, and any other must-haves. Don't include luxuries; sushi nights and streaming subscriptions don't count. Once you've got a total, multiply that by how many months you want your safety net to cover. If your monthly burn is $1,000 and you're aiming for a three-month fund, you'll need $3,000 stashed away. This number isn't static, though. Life changes, and so should your emergency fund. Regularly revisiting your calculations ensures your fund keeps pace with your life.

Starting Small: Building Your Fund Bit by Bit

The idea of saving thousands might sound like climbing Everest in flip-flops, especially if you're not swimming in cash. But here's the kicker—you don't have to fund this overnight. Starting small is perfectly fine. The key is consistency. Even a small amount, say $50 from each paycheck, begins to build momentum over time. Consider setting up an automatic transfer to a dedicated emergency savings account each payday. It's out of your hands before you can even think about spending it, padding your emergency fund without pinching your lifestyle.

Keeping It Accessible: Smart Storage for Your Emergency Fund

Now, let's talk about where to park this fund. Accessibility is crucial —you don't want your funds locked up when you need them most. However, too easy access can be a temptation trap, leading you to dip into it for non-emergencies. A high-yield savings account strikes a good balance. It keeps your money separate from your day-to-day funds but accessible enough that you can get to it quickly when needed. Plus, it earns a bit of interest, helping your emergency fund grow passively.

Moreover, resist the urge to invest your emergency fund in the stock market. High returns might sound enticing, but the market's volatility could shrink your fund just when you need it most. Stick to options where your money is protected and the value doesn't fluctuate, ensuring that every penny you save is ready to protect you when the storm hits.

Jake, a 25-year-old recent college graduate, established an emergency fund after getting his first job. He calculated his monthly expenses and set a goal to save $4,500 for a three-month buffer. By setting aside $100 from each paycheck into a high-yield savings account, Jake gradually built up his fund. When his car suddenly broke down, requiring costly repairs, Jake was able to use his emergency fund to cover the expenses without stress. This financial safety net allowed him to handle the unexpected cost smoothly, providing him with peace of mind even when life was unpredictable.

By steadily building and smartly positioning your emergency fund, you create a financial bulwark that shields you from life's unforeseen expenses. Whether it's a medical emergency, urgent home repairs, or an abrupt job loss, your emergency fund is your first line of financial defense, ensuring that these shocks don't derail your financial stability or long-term goals. Instead of scrambling in panic, you'll handle life's surprises with a calm confidence, secure in the knowledge that your finances are under control, no matter what happens.

In the next chapter, we dive deeper into the world of credit and debt management—a crucial arena for anyone looking to build a solid financial foundation. Before we depart the topic of saving, though, look through this checklist for a quick refresher on the key ideas.

ACTION STEPS FOR MASTERING MONEY SAVING TECHNIQUES

1. Prioritize Savings

- Set a savings goal (e.g., 5% of income).
- Adjust your savings rate as your income increases.

2. Utilize Compound Interest

- Open a high-yield savings account.
- Regularly deposit money to benefit from compound interest.

3. Find Extra Money to Save

- Audit expenses for unnecessary costs.
- Follow frugal living tips and find deals.

4. Establish Your Emergency Fund

- Aim for 3-6 months' living expenses.
- Use a high-yield savings account.

CHAPTER 4

CREDIT AND DEBT MANAGEMENT

Debt erases freedom more surely than anything else.

MARRYN SOMERSET WEBB

Understanding the difference between good debt and bad debt is essential for sound financial management. Good debt refers to borrowing that can enhance your financial future, such as student loans, mortgages, or business loans. In these cases, the borrowed funds are used to invest in assets that have the potential to grow in value or generate income. Conversely, bad debt usually means borrowing money for things that lose value quickly or aren't really necessary. This includes using credit cards for everyday shopping or taking out expensive loans for things you don't really need. This kind of debt doesn't help your financial situation, and it can often trap you in a cycle of paying off more and more debt. Recognizing and differentiating between these types of debt can help you make smarter financial decisions and build a more secure economic future.

4.1 BUILDING CREDIT FROM SCRATCH: MORE THAN JUST A NUMBER

A credit score, in its essence, is a measure of your creditworthiness. Once you move out of your parent's house, your credit score will be a silent companion for the rest of your life. It can help you or hurt you, and it all depends on the financial choices you make. Banks and lenders use this number to decide if lending you money is a risky bet or a safe one. This score is calculated based on your financial behaviors—like those times you paid (or didn't pay) your bills on time, the mountain (or molehill) of debt you owe, and the length of your credit history. This is where being a financial "newbie" can be a bit of a disadvantage. Lenders love a long, positive track record because it gives them a sense of your good money management habits over time.

Your credit score is a number that ranges typically from 300 to 850. The higher your score, the more financially trustworthy you are perceived to be.

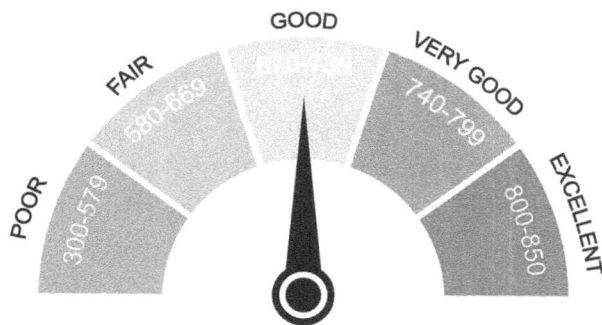

CREDIT SCORE

Why does this number matter? Your credit score influences your ability to borrow money, secure a place to live, and sometimes even land a job. It can also affect your insurance rates, security deposits on rentals, and even your eligibility for cell phone contracts.

A good credit score can mean lower interest rates when you borrow money, translating to thousands of dollars saved over time. On the flip side, a low score can lead to higher interest rates, hefty security deposits, or outright rejections. Britton and Adam both borrowed $10,000 to buy their first car. With good credit, Britton pays $181.92 per month for his car loan, totaling $10,915.20 over five years. Adam, with bad credit, pays $222.44 per month, totaling $13,346.40 over the same period. Due to his lower credit score, Adam pays $40.52 more per month and $2,431.20 more than Britton over the life of the loan. When we say that having good credit will save you a lot of money, we really mean it!

Starting Points for Building Credit: Planting the Seeds

Building credit might seem like a catch-22—you need credit to build credit. So, where do you begin? One of the safest starting points is with a secured credit card. This is a type of credit card that's backed by a cash deposit from you, which typically sets your credit limit. Think of it as training wheels for credit usage; it helps you build your score without the risk of falling into debt, provided you manage it responsibly.

Student credit cards are another great option, especially designed for young adults like you. They typically have lower credit limits and more lenient approval criteria, tailored to those with little to no credit history. Some even offer rewards like cash back on groceries or gas, making them not only a tool for building credit but also for saving on everyday expenses.

Responsible Credit Habits: The Building Blocks

Once you've got your credit card, it's about spending wisely. The golden rule? Always pay your bills on time! Late payments can knock points off your credit score faster than you can say "due date." Set up reminders or automate your payments to dodge this bullet. Also, pay off your credit card every single month. Credit card interest rates are no joke (We're talking between 18% and 29% or even higher.), so only spend as much as you can easily pay at the end of the month.

When it comes to your credit rating, there's the amount you owe, which sounds straightforward but has a twist. It's not just how much you owe; it's how much you owe compared to your available credit, a ratio known as your "credit utilization." Maxing out your credit cards is a red flag to lenders, signaling potential desperation. A good rule of thumb is to keep your utilization under 30%. For example, if your credit limit is $1,000, try to keep the balance you owe below $300.

Monitoring and Understanding Your Credit Report: Your Financial Mirror

Once a year, you can get a free credit report from the three major credit reporting bureaus—Equifax, Experian, and TransUnion. It's like an annual check-up for your financial health. Here's a quick checklist to guide you through reviewing your credit report:

1. **Confirm Your Personal Info**: Ensure your name, address, and employment information are correct.
2. **Review Credit Accounts**: Verify that all accounts listed are yours and that the details, like balances and payment histories, are accurate.

3. **Spot Errors and Fraud**: Look for any accounts you don't recognize or errors in reporting. These could be signs of fraud or mistakes dragging down your score.
4. **Plan Corrections**: If you find errors, report them immediately to the credit bureau and the institution that provided the incorrect information.

Understanding and regularly checking your credit report empowers you to take control of your credit score. It allows you to spot issues early and to track how your financial behaviors affect your credit over time. Just as you wouldn't ignore a check engine light in your car, don't ignore your credit report. It's an important tool in maintaining and improving your financial health.

By grasping the importance of your credit score, you're laying down a solid financial foundation. Things like using the right financial tools, adopting responsible credit habits, and regularly monitoring your credit report are your stepping stones through the world of credit to survive and thrive. They will enable you to leverage your financial reputation to achieve your personal and financial goals.

Let's look at the stories of Jason and Mark, two best friends who grew up as neighbors. As they ventured into adulthood, their paths toward financial understanding diverged significantly.

Jason, always meticulous and forward-thinking, understood the importance of a strong credit history early on. He applied for his first credit card during college, using it strictly for necessary purchases and paying the balance in full each month. By the time he graduated, he had already established a respectable credit score.

On the other hand, Mark, easygoing and spontaneous, rarely considered the long-term implications of his financial decisions. He had little understanding of how credit worked and did not see the urgency in learning about it. Utilities and other bills were often paid late when he remembered them at the last minute. The concept of a credit score was foreign to him, so he never bothered to check his score until it became necessary.

The day came when both friends, now in their late twenties, decided to buy homes in their hometown. Jason approached the bank with confidence, armed with a strong credit score and a substantial down payment saved from years of careful financial planning. The bank offered him a favorable mortgage rate, making his dream of owning a home a smooth reality.

Mark's experience, however, was starkly different. Upon applying for a mortgage, he was shocked to find his credit score was poor. The bank explained how his habitual late payments and lack of credit history had negatively impacted his score. As a result, he faced high interest rates that he hadn't anticipated, and the loan terms offered were far from favorable. Struggling to secure a mortgage, Mark realized that he had to delay his plans for homeownership and instead work on repairing his credit, which meant months, if not years, of diligent attention to his finances.

Their contrasting experiences reinforced the value of financial literacy and planning. While Jason enjoyed the comfort of his new home, Mark embarked on a journey to rebuild his financial health, hopeful that one day, he, too, would be ready to step into a home of his own.

4.2 FINANCIAL STRATEGIES FOR COLLEGE: MINIMIZING DEBT

While education costs can be considered "good debt" because you are investing in your future earning potential, getting a degree with little or no debt at all is even better. College students have many avenues for finding scholarships and grants to offset tuition costs. Here are some of the best ways:

1. **College Financial Aid Offices**: Start by contacting your college's financial aid office. They can provide information on institutional scholarships and grants offered by the college itself and guidance on how to apply for external scholarships.
2. **Scholarship Search Engines**: Utilize online scholarship search engines such as *Fastweb*, *Scholarships.com*, and *College Board's Scholarship Search*. These platforms allow you to create a profile and match you with scholarships that fit your background, interests, and qualifications.
3. **Community Organizations and Foundations**: Many community organizations, foundations, and local businesses offer scholarships to students in their area. Check with community centers, religious organizations, Rotary Clubs, and other local groups to inquire about scholarship opportunities.
4. **Professional Associations**: If you're pursuing a specific field of study or career path, look for opportunities offered by professional associations related to that field. These organizations often provide scholarships to support students pursuing careers in their industry.
5. **Employer and Parental Benefits**: Some employers offer tuition assistance programs for employees or their dependents. Check with your employer or parent's employer to explore these options. Additionally, family members of veterans or active-duty military service personnel may be eligible for educational benefits through programs such as the GI Bill.

6. **Government Grants and Programs**: Explore government-funded grants and programs, such as the Pell Grant for undergraduate students with financial need or state-specific grants and scholarships. Visit the Federal Student Aid website (fafsa.gov) for information on federal grants and how to apply.

7. **Online Platforms and Crowdfunding**: Consider using online crowdfunding platforms like GoFundMe or crowdfunding features on scholarship websites to raise funds for your education. Share your story and goals to attract donors who may be willing to support your educational expenses.

8. **Essay Contests and Competitions**: Keep an eye out for essay contests, competitions, and other opportunities that offer scholarships as prizes. Many organizations and companies sponsor contests on various topics, providing scholarships to winners.

9. **High School Guidance Counselors**: If you're still in high school, reach out to your guidance counselor for assistance in finding and applying for scholarships. They may have resources and information on local and national scholarships available to graduating seniors.

10. **Online Research and Networking**: Conduct thorough online research and network with peers, mentors, and educators to uncover lesser-known scholarship opportunities. Stay proactive and persistent in your search efforts to maximize your chances of securing financial aid.

Remember that even if you have already started college, you can continue to apply for scholarships until you graduate. The time you spend searching for and applying for scholarships will pay for itself. Even if you aren't the smartest kid in the class or a successful college athlete, there are plenty of scholarships for everyone.

4.3 STUDENT LOANS: BORROWING WISELY AND REPAYMENT STRATEGIES

Perhaps you've got some scholarships and/or grant money, and you're working hard at a part-time job, but it still won't be enough to cover everything. Now what? When borrowing money for college, aim for a loan amount that you can comfortably repay based on your future earning potential. A common guideline is to ensure that your total student loan debt does not exceed your expected annual starting salary after graduation. This can help prevent overwhelming debt burdens and make your loan payments manageable.

As for the "magic ratio" of future earning potential to the loan amount, there isn't a specific universal formula since it can vary widely depending on individual circumstances, such as career choice, earning potential in specific fields, and personal financial goals. However, a commonly suggested guideline is to aim for a debt-to-income ratio (the ratio of your total monthly debt payments to your gross monthly income) of 36% or lower. Remember that this includes all your debt, not just student loans.

To determine how much you can make in different fields, you can research average salaries and earning potential for various careers. There are several resources you can use:

1. **Bureau of Labor Statistics (BLS)**: The BLS provides comprehensive data on employment, wages, and projections for various occupations in the United States. You can find detailed information on median salaries, job outlook, and educational requirements for different professions.
2. **Salary Websites**: Websites like *Glassdoor*, *PayScale*, and *Indeed* offer salary data based on user-reported salaries and employer-reported salary ranges. These platforms can

provide insights into the average salaries for specific job titles and industries.

3. **Career Services**: Many colleges and universities have departments providing resources and guidance on career exploration, job search strategies, and salary negotiation. They may offer access to salary surveys or alumni data to help you understand earning potential in different fields.

4. **Professional Associations**: Industry-specific professional associations often conduct salary surveys and publish reports on compensation trends within their respective fields. Joining these associations or accessing their resources online can provide valuable insights into salary expectations for different occupations.

By researching salary data and considering your career goals and financial circumstances, you can make informed decisions about how much to borrow for college and which career paths may offer the best return on your investment.

It's tempting to view student loans as free money but remember that this is a loan—not a gift. You'll need to pay back every dime, with a hearty side of interest, even if you drop out before getting your degree. Start by breaking down your college expenses: tuition, books, housing, food, and, yes, even some cash for fun. Then, subtract any scholarships, grants, and part-time job earnings. The goal here isn't to fund a lavish college lifestyle but to cover your necessities. A practical approach is to budget strictly and to borrow conservatively. Consider used or electronic textbooks, opt for a less expensive meal plan, or choose budget-friendly housing. Every dollar you don't borrow is one you won't have to pay back with interest later.

When choosing between federal and private loans, think of it as choosing between a fixed-rate mortgage and an adjustable-rate mortgage.

- **Federal loans** are like the fixed-rate option. They're generally safer, with fixed interest rates and more flexible repayment options. They also come with benefits like deferment, forbearance, and access to various repayment plans, including income-driven repayment plans that adjust your monthly payments based on your income.
- **Private loans**, on the other hand, can be more like an adjustable-rate mortgage. They might offer lower interest rates initially, but those rates can fluctuate. Also, they often require a credit check. Additionally, private loans don't usually offer the same breadth of repayment options and protections as federal loans. They're more rigid, and if you find yourself struggling financially, you might not have as much wiggle room.

When it comes to repayment, let's talk strategy. Once you're out of college, you'll likely look at many repayment plans. Here's where it gets really personal. You'll need to pick a plan that suits your financial situation and your stress tolerance. Standard repayment plans will generally have you debt-free faster, but the payments can be hefty. Graduated repayment plans start with lower payments that increase over time, hopefully alongside your salary. Then there's the income-driven repayment, which adjusts your monthly payments based on your income and family size, often extending the life of your loan but reducing monthly payments.

For those entering public service, loan forgiveness might sound like a financial fairy godmother. Programs like Public Service Loan Forgiveness (PSLF) can erase remaining debt after 10 years of qualifying payments for those working in government, non-profit, or other qualifying public service jobs. However, this program has a maze of eligibility requirements—from the type of loans you have to the specifics of your employment contract—making it crucial to ensure you're ticking all the right boxes from the get-go.

Navigating student loans is no walk in the park, but with a clear understanding of your needs, careful borrowing, choosing the right type of loan, and strategizing your repayment, you can manage your education debt without letting it manage you. Remember that the decisions you make about student loans can impact your financial landscape far into the future. Therefore, consider your options carefully, plan with precision, and, when in doubt, reach out to a financial advisor. You are setting up a financial foundation that will support you well beyond your college years.

Financial Success Stories and Cautionary Tales: Lessons in College Financial Management

Students with Too Much Student Debt:

1. Drake: Drake graduated with a degree in art history and accumulated $100,000 in student loan debt. Due to a competitive job market and lower earning potential in the field, Drake struggled to find a job that paid more than $30,000 per year. With a debt burden far exceeding his annual income, Drake faced significant challenges in managing loan payments while covering basic living expenses.
2. Sarah: Sarah pursued a graduate degree in a specialized field, taking out $150,000 in student loans to finance her education. Despite completing her program and securing a job in her field, Sarah's starting salary was lower than anticipated due to unexpected industry dynamics and the fact that she was offered only entry-level positions. With a debt-to-income ratio well above the recommended levels,

Sarah found herself financially strained and unable to make meaningful progress in paying down her student debt.

Students with Manageable Student Debt:

1. Marcus: Marcus attended a public university and carefully managed his finances throughout college. He received scholarships and grants, worked part-time during the school year, and interned during the summers to gain experience in his field. By graduation, Marcus had accumulated only $20,000 in student loans. After securing a job in his field with a starting salary of $50,000 per year, Marcus was able to comfortably manage his loan payments while still saving for the future.

2. Sophia: Sophia chose to attend a community college for the first two years of her undergraduate education to save on tuition costs. She then transferred to a four-year university to complete her degree, minimizing her student loan debt. By graduation, Sophia owed $30,000 in student loans. With a degree in a high-demand field and a starting salary of $60,000 per year, Sophia's debt-to-income ratio remained manageable, allowing her to make steady progress in repaying her loans while maintaining a comfortable standard of living.

These examples illustrate the importance of considering earning potential, loan amounts, and financial management strategies when making decisions about student loan borrowing. By choosing fields with solid job prospects and being strategic and proactive in managing finances during college, students can minimize their debt burdens and achieve financial stability after graduation.

4.4 THE TRUTH ABOUT CREDIT CARDS: BENEFITS AND TRAPS

Navigating credit card offers can feel a bit like decoding an ancient script—full of terms and conditions that seem designed to confuse rather than clarify. Let's decode some of these cryptic messages, starting with the ever-present APR, or Annual Percentage Rate. Picture APR as the price tag of borrowing money on your credit card. It's the rate at which interest will pile up on any balances, or the amount you still owe that carries over from month to month. Lower APRs are like finding a designer jacket on clearance—it means less debt accumulating each month you don't pay off your full balance.

Then, there are annual fees and rewards programs. Annual fees are straightforward—it's what you pay each year to use the card. Whether this fee is worth it often hinges on the rewards program linked to the card. Rewards programs can offer travel miles, cash back, or points redeemable at various retailers. Here's the kicker: if you're paying a hefty annual fee to earn rewards, you need to be sure you're actually getting more in rewards value than you're shelling out. It's like buying a gym membership—if you're not going often enough to justify the cost, it's money down the drain.

Now, let's talk about the double-edged sword of compound interest. When it works in your favor, such as in a high-yield savings account, it's like having a golden goose that lays golden eggs. But in the world of credit card debt, it's more like an unpleasant snowball rolling downhill, growing bigger and faster as it goes. Here's how it plays out. You don't pay off the entire amount, so you carry a balance owed, and interest is charged. Next month, you get charged interest not only on the original amount owed but also on the interest that was added the previous month. This continues month after month. Before you know it, what started as a manageable amount can balloon into a daunting debt.

Navigating this terrain requires a map and some savvy travel tips. For starters, always strive to pay off the card in full each month. If this is too much, try to pay more than the minimum. Minimum payments are like putting a Band-Aid on a leaky pipe—they're a temporary fix that doesn't solve the problem and often ends up costing more in the long run. By paying only the minimum, you mainly pay off the interest, not the principal. That means it takes longer and costs more to clear your debt. Let's look at Kendra, who had $1,000 of credit card debt with 18% interest. She made the minimum monthly payments for two years but was shocked to discover that she still owed $886.55 after 24 payments totaling $453.39. Have you ever run on a treadmill? This is what Kendra was doing. She was putting in the effort but not actually moving forward. Clearing debt from credit cards will save you hundreds, if not thousands, of dollars and should be a top priority.

Late fees are another pitfall. Miss a payment deadline, and you're not just facing a fee. Your interest rate could skyrocket, and your credit score might take a hit. Setting up reminders or automating your payments can keep you on track and out of the late fee trap.

Maximizing the benefits of credit cards without falling into debt is akin to playing a strategic game where planning moves ahead is crucial. Use your card for regular purchases you'd make anyway and have the cash to cover, like groceries or gas. This way, you earn rewards without spending extra. Then, pay off the balance in full each month. This strategy requires discipline but pays off by building your credit score, avoiding interest, and accumulating rewards—all without accruing debt.

Credit cards are tests of your financial discipline. Used wisely, they can be powerful allies in building your credit and reaping rewards. But without careful management, they can become quicksand for your finances, pulling you into a debt spiral that's tough to escape.

Like any powerful tool, the key lies in knowing how to wield it to your advantage—maximizing benefits while sidestepping the traps set along the way.

4.5 MANAGING DEBT WITHOUT DERAILING YOUR DREAMS

We hope that after reading this book, you will never find yourself in crippling debt, but sometimes life happens, and it's good to have a few skills up your sleeves to get you out of money trouble. Your financial dreams might feel more like distant fairy tales when you're deep in debt. Here's the secret: with the right strategies and a bit of grit, you can navigate out of debt and back on the path to achieving your dreams. Let's explore two popular methods to tackle debt: the **Debt Snowball** and **Debt Avalanche** methods.

- The **Debt Snowball** method is like training for a marathon by first running a lap around your block. You start with your smallest debt, regardless of interest rate, and pay as much as you can toward it while maintaining minimum payments on other debts. Once that first debt is out of the picture, you take the amount you were paying on it and add it to the minimum payment on your next smallest debt. This process creates a "snowball effect" as each debt gets eliminated, and your available capital for the next one increases. It's psychologically gratifying—seeing debts disappear quickly boosts your morale, keeping you motivated.
- Contrast this with the **Debt Avalanche** method, which might be likened to tackling the steepest part of the climb first. Here, you prioritize debts with the highest interest rates, regardless of the balance. You make minimum payments on all other debts and use any remaining funds to

clear the costliest debt first. This method can save you money in the long term because you're reducing the amount of high-interest debt faster. However, it requires patience since it might take longer to see your first debt fully paid off, which can be a motivational challenge.

Negotiating with creditors can also be a game-changer in your debt repayment strategy. Think of it as seeking a truce with your opponents. It's possible to negotiate lower interest rates or settlement amounts. Start by reviewing your financial situation thoroughly; knowing exactly what you can afford to pay is crucial. Approach your creditors with honesty and clarity about your situation. Many are willing to consider lower interest rates, extended payment terms, or even reducing the principal amount if it increases the likelihood of repayment. Being proactive and transparent can lead to more manageable repayment terms.

Maintaining an emergency fund plays a critical role in debt management. It's your financial safety net, designed to catch you in case of unexpected expenses without further sinking into debt. Without it, any sudden expense—be it a car repair or a medical bill—can force you back into the debt cycle. Aim to build and keep an emergency fund that covers at least three to six months of living expenses. This fund ensures that you can stick to your debt repayment plan without interruption, providing peace of mind as you work toward becoming debt-free.

Lifestyle changes are often necessary to accelerate debt repayment. This might mean re-evaluating your spending habits—dining out less frequently, cutting down on shopping sprees, or opting for more cost-effective entertainment options. Each dollar saved can be redirected toward paying off your debt. Also, consider ways to increase your income—taking on freelance work, a part-time job, or selling items you no longer need. The additional cash flow can significantly speed up your debt repayment timeline.

Staying motivated throughout this journey is critical. Debt repayment can be a long and challenging road, and it's easy to feel disheartened. Keep your goals in sight—remind yourself why you're working hard to get out of debt, whether it's buying a home, investing in your education, or simply enjoying a stress-free life. Celebrate small victories along the way. Each debt cleared is a step closer to your financial independence. Stay connected with supportive friends or online communities who are also working toward similar financial goals. Their encouragement and advice can be invaluable as you navigate your way out of debt.

As this chapter on managing debt concludes, remember that the path out of debt is traveled one step at a time. By choosing the right strategy, whether it's the snowball or avalanche method, negotiating wisely with creditors, maintaining an emergency fund, making smart lifestyle choices, and keeping your spirits high, you are setting yourself up for success. These efforts will not only help you manage and overcome your debt, but also empower you to rebuild and reclaim your financial freedom.

ACTION STEPS FOR CREDIT AND DEBT MANAGEMENT

1. Build and Maintain a Good Credit Score

- Apply for a secured credit card or a student credit card to start building credit.
- Always pay your bills on time to avoid late payments.
- Keep your credit utilization below 30%.

2. Monitor Your Credit Report Regularly

- Obtain a free credit report annually from each of the three major credit bureaus.
- Verify that all personal information and account details are accurate.
- Report any errors or signs of fraud immediately.

3. Strategize for Minimizing College Debt

- Apply for scholarships and grants through college financial aid offices, community organizations, and sources found through online search engines.
- Utilize tuition assistance programs from employers or parental benefits.
- Borrow conservatively and focus on necessary expenses.

4. Manage Student Loans Wisely

- Aim for a loan amount that does not exceed your expected annual starting salary.
- Choose federal loans for their fixed interest rates and flexible repayment options.
- Explore repayment plans and loan forgiveness programs that best fit your financial situation.

5. Use Credit Cards Responsibly

- Pay off your credit card balance in full each month to avoid interest charges.
- Avoid carrying a high balance relative to your credit limit.
- Set up payment reminders or automate payments to prevent late fees.

6. Develop Debt Repayment Strategies

- Consider the Debt Snowball method to quickly eliminate small debts for a motivational boost.
- Use the Debt Avalanche method to save money by paying off high-interest debts first.
- Negotiate with creditors for lower interest rates or more manageable repayment terms.

7. Maintain an Emergency Fund

- Save three to six months' worth of living expenses to handle unexpected costs without accruing more debt.
- Keep the fund in a high-yield savings account for easy access and growth.

MAKE A DIFFERENCE WITH YOUR REVIEW
UNLOCK THE POWER OF GENEROSITY

"Helping one person might not change the whole world, but it could change the world for one person."

People who give without expectation live longer, happier lives and often find more success. So if we've got a shot at that during our time together, let's make it happen.

Our mission is to make financial literacy accessible to everyone. Everything we do stems from that mission. And the only way for us to accomplish that mission is by reaching...well...everyone.

This is where you come in. Most people do, in fact, judge a book by its cover (and its reviews). So here's my ask on behalf of a struggling teen or young adult you've never met:

Please help that young reader by leaving this book a review.

Your gift costs no money and takes less than 60 seconds but can change someone's life forever.

Scan the QR code to leave your review on Amazon

If you feel good about helping a faceless young adult, you are my kind of person. Welcome to the club. You're one of us.

Thank you from the bottom of my heart. Now, back to our regularly scheduled programming.

https://amzn.to/472gr69

CHAPTER 5
INVESTING FOR BEGINNERS

Investing is not nearly as difficult as it looks. Successful investing involves doing a few things right and avoiding serious mistakes.

JACK BOGLE

So, you've saved up some cash, and now you're staring at your bank balance, thinking, "What's next?" It's like being all dressed up with nowhere to go. Welcome to the world of investing, where your money doesn't just sit there looking pretty—it gets to work, potentially multiplying like rabbits in the spring. Let's demystify this whole investing concept, starting from the basics and ensuring you won't feel like you're trying to read a map upside down.

5.1 YOUR FIRST INVESTMENT: STARTING SMALL

The Power of Micro-Investing: Big Dreams From Small Starts

Imagine if saving for your investment portfolio was as easy as rounding up your smoothie purchase and tossing the spare change into a growing money mountain. That's micro-investing—no need for big lump sums, just steady trickles that build up over time. It's perfect if you're not ready to dive into the deep end with large amounts of cash. Think of it like planting seeds in various pots— some might grow more than others, but all you need to start is a little soil and a few seeds, so you're not out very much over those that don't do well.

Micro-investing platforms have sprouted up all over, making it ridiculously easy to start. They work by rounding up your purchases to the nearest dollar and investing the difference. So, when you buy a burger for $5.75, that extra 25 cents gets invested. Over time, and with enough burgers, those quarters build a respectable portfolio. It's investing at a snail's pace, but remember that even snails reach the finish line.

Choosing the Right Platforms: Where to Plant Your Money Seeds

Not all micro-investing platforms are created equal, and choosing where to park your hard-earned cash can feel as daunting as picking a film on movie night. What should you look for?

Start with fees. Some apps charge monthly fees, while others take a percentage of your portfolio. It's like a cover charge at a club, so make sure it's worth what you're getting.

Next, consider features. Some apps offer automatic rebalancing, while others let you pick specific stocks or funds. Think about how much control you want and how much you're willing to learn.

User experience is also key. An app that's a nightmare to navigate can be a dealbreaker. Look for intuitive design and clear instructions. It's supposed to make investing easier, not give you a headache.

Lastly, check out reviews and ratings. They can provide insights into reliability and customer satisfaction. It's like checking a new movie's rating before you decide to watch it in the theater.

Automating Investments: Set It, Forget It, Let It Grow

If micro-investing is the first step, automating your investments is the power walk. By setting up automatic transfers to your investment account, you ensure consistent growth without thinking about it. It's like a gym membership for your wealth—regular workouts without requiring you to set reminders to hit the gym. Most platforms allow you to set up weekly, biweekly, or monthly transfers so you can tailor the flow to match your income cycle.

This approach taps into the magic of dollar-cost averaging. This means you invest a fixed amount regularly, regardless of the market's ups and downs. Sometimes, you'll buy when prices are high, and other times when they're low. Over time, these averages work out to potentially lower the cost of investing. It's like buying your favorite snacks, whether on sale or not, because you know you'll eat them eventually.

Risk and Return: Balancing Act on a Tightrope

Investing isn't just about watching your money grow; it's about managing how much uncertainty you can stomach. Micro-investing generally involves smaller amounts, so while the dollar risk is low, the percentage risk can be high, especially if you're dipping toes into volatile markets. Understanding this balance is crucial. Most apps provide some guidance, but doing a bit of homework on risk tolerance can save you some nail-biting moments.

Think about how you'd feel if you woke up to find your investment halved. If that thought gives you a cold sweat, you might want to stick to safer, albeit potentially lower-return options. Conversely, if you're the financial equivalent of a thrill-seeker, you might be okay with riskier investments that offer higher returns. Knowing where you stand on this spectrum is key to making investment choices that won't keep you up at night.

Setting Investment Goals: Your Financial Roadmap

Investment goals are your financial destination. Without them, you're just wandering through the wilderness of options without a clear path. Start by defining what you're investing for. Is it a big trip? A new car? Retirement? Each goal might require a different investment strategy and timeline. Short-term goals usually need safer investments that are easy to access quickly, while you can afford to be more aggressive with long-term goals if you have time to ride out market fluctuations.

Once your goals are set, consider how much risk you're willing to take and how much you need to invest regularly to meet your goals. This might require some adjustments along the way as your goals or financial situation changes, but having a clear blueprint from the start can make the journey less daunting and a lot more rewarding. Remember that every investor started somewhere, and with these steps, you're already on your way to growing your wealth. Take a deep breath, and let's dive into the world of investments, where your money doesn't just sit idle—it grows, changes, and ultimately works for you, paving the way toward financial independence and security.

5.2 NAVIGATING THE STOCK MARKET: FIRST-TIME INVESTOR'S GUIDE

So, you've decided to try the stock market, where fortunes can be made and, yes, sometimes lost. Before you dive in, let's get a lay of the land, or rather, a lay of the market. Essentially, the stock market is where the magic of buying and selling shares of companies happens. Think of it as a giant, complex network where everyone from big-time investors to everyday folks come to trade pieces of businesses. These shares represent a slice of ownership in a company. When you buy a share, you're betting on the company's future success. If the company does well, the value of your shares might increase, and if it doesn't, the opposite happens.

Understanding this marketplace's role in the economy is important. It's more than individual gains; the stock market is a barometer of economic health. When the market is up, it often reflects confidence in the economy. Companies use the capital (money collected from selling shares) to innovate, expand, and hire more people, fueling economic growth. Conversely, a downturn might indicate economic troubles on the horizon. Investing in the stock market is a bit like planting a garden in your community; you're contributing to and benefiting from the economic ecosystem.

Now, let's talk about how you actually read this market. You're not alone if you've ever glanced at a stock chart and felt like you were trying to read hieroglyphics. Stock charts can look intimidating, with their lines, bars, and colors, but they're really just a way to track the performance of a stock over time. The most common type is the line chart or line graph, showing the closing price of a stock over a set period. What you're looking for are trends—does the stock generally go up, or does it steadily fall? Is it volatile, with big peaks and troughs, or stable? Learning to read these charts can help you make more informed decisions about when to buy or sell.

Several reliable platforms and websites offer comprehensive charting tools. Some popular options are *Yahoo Finance*, *Google Finance*, *TradingView*, *Bloomberg*, *MarketWatch*, and *MSN Money*.

Understanding diversification is your next step. There's an old saying, "Don't put all your eggs in one basket," and it couldn't be truer in the world of investing. Diversification is about spreading your investments across various assets—different stocks, industries, and even types of investments, like bonds or real estate. This strategy helps mitigate risk. If one investment tanks, others in different sectors or asset classes might hold steady or even increase. Think of it as a financial safety net, allowing you to manage potential losses more smoothly without it being a total wipeout.

For beginners, knowing whether to go long or short is like deciding whether you're in for a marathon or a sprint. Long-term investment strategies involve buying stocks with the intention of holding onto them for years or even decades. You're looking for companies you believe will grow steadily over time, benefiting from the wonders of compound growth. On the other hand, short-term strategies might involve buying and selling stocks over a shorter period, capitalizing on market fluctuations. Both approaches have their merits and risks, and your choice should align with your financial goals, timeline, and, importantly, your comfort with risk.

Navigating the stock market is an exhilarating part of building your investment portfolio. It requires patience, a cool head, and a willing-ness to learn continuously. Whether you're looking at trends on a stock chart, picking a diverse set of investments, or deciding on your investment timeline, each step you take is building your competence and confidence in handling market dynamics. Remember that every investor started somewhere, and each had their first encounter with a stock chart, their first trade, and their first lesson in diversification. By starting small, staying informed, and sticking to your strategy, you're well on your way to becoming a savvy market participant.

5.3 BONDS, MUTUAL FUNDS, AND ETFS: WHAT'S RIGHT FOR YOU?

Understanding Bonds: Your Portfolio's Safety Net

Think of bonds as the chill, reliable friends in your investment circle —the ones you invite over when you need a break from the high-energy, unpredictable ones (I'm looking at you, stocks.). Bonds are essentially loans you give to governments or corporations, and in return, they promise to pay you back on a fixed schedule with interest. It's like lending money to a friend who insists on paying you back with a little extra for your trust.

There are a few different types of bonds to choose from, each with its own level of "chill." Government bonds are considered super safe; they're backed by the government, which makes them the equivalent of your friend who always shows up on time. Then there are corporate bonds, which are a bit riskier but offer higher interest rates, kind of like that friend who's a blast to hang out with but sometimes cancels at the last minute. Municipal bonds are another option, generally safe with the perk of being tax-exempt, making them the financially savvy friend of the group.

Integrating bonds into your portfolio can be a smart move, especially if you're the type who likes a bit of predictability in your financial life. They provide a steady income through interest payments, and because they're generally less volatile than stocks, they can help smooth out the bumps when the stock market gets a bit too wild. It's about balance—having enough excitement to keep things interesting but enough stability not to lose sleep over your investments.

Mutual Funds Explained: Pooling for Power

Now, let's talk mutual funds, which are like going in on a giant potluck dinner. Everyone brings a dish (or in this case, money), and you all get to share in a diverse feast of investments that none of you could have whipped up on your own. Managed by professionals who decide which stocks, bonds, or other assets to invest in, mutual funds allow you to own a small piece of a big portfolio.

The beauty of mutual funds lies in their diversity. They naturally spread out your risk because they invest in a broad range of assets. It's like diversifying your dinner spread; if the lasagna turns out a bit bland, there's still chicken, salad, and dessert to enjoy. For you, as an investor, this means that if one investment in the fund dips, the others might still be performing well, which can help buffer against losses.

Mutual funds are particularly appealing for new investors because they handle the heavy lifting. You don't need to research every stock or bond; the fund manager does that for you. Plus, because you're pooling resources with other investors, you can get started with relatively small amounts of money. It's a way to get a taste of a large, diversified portfolio without the hefty price tag or the hassle of managing it yourself.

ETFs for Beginners: The Flexible Investment

Exchange-Traded Funds (ETFs) are like mutual funds' trendy cousins. They also pool money from many investors to buy a diversified portfolio, but with a twist—they trade on stock exchanges, just like individual stocks. This means you can buy and sell shares of

ETFs throughout the trading day at market price. Imagine grabbing a plate from the potluck anytime you want, not just when the dinner starts or ends.

One of the biggest advantages of ETFs is their flexibility. Because they trade like stocks, you have more control over when you buy or sell, and you can often do it with lower investment fees than you'll have to pay on traditional mutual funds. It's an efficient way to diversify your investments and a fantastic tool for new investors who want both diversity and flexibility.

Choosing Investments for Your Goals: Aligning Your Financial Compass

When you're faced with the choice between bonds, mutual funds, and ETFs, how do you make the right decision? Start with your goals and timeline. If you're saving for a short-term goal, like a big trip in a couple of years, you might lean toward more stable investments like bonds or bond ETFs, which reduce the risk of major changes in value. For long-term goals like retirement, you might look toward mutual funds or stock ETFs, which can offer higher growth potential over time.

Also, consider your appetite for risk and how much time you want to spend managing your investments. If you prefer a set-it-and-forget-it approach, mutual funds managed by professionals can be a great choice. If you like having more control and the ability to make quick changes, ETFs might be more your style. If security is your top priority, traditional bonds can provide that steady, reliable investment you might be looking for.

As you navigate through these options, think of yourself as a chef in a well-stocked kitchen. Each ingredient—bonds, mutual funds, ETFs—has its role to play in your financial recipe. By understanding what each one brings to the table and how they align with your financial taste and goals, you can mix and match them to create a portfolio that's nutritious for your financial health and deliciously rewarding.

5.4 NAVIGATING CRYPTOCURRENCY: WHAT YOUNG ADULTS SHOULD KNOW

Cryptocurrency Basics: Diving into the Digital Coin Pool

Let's start by unpacking the enigma that is cryptocurrency, often just called crypto, because who isn't into a good nickname? Cryptocurrency is a type of digital money that only exists online. Unlike regular money, which banks and governments control, cryptocurrency is decentralized, meaning it's managed by a network of computers around the world. These computers use special technology called blockchain to keep track of all transactions. Think of blockchain as a digital notebook where every page records transactions. Once a page is full, it gets added to the end of the notebook, and everyone involved gets an identical copy of this notebook. Because each new page is connected to the previous one, and everyone has the same copy, it's almost impossible to change anything without everyone noticing. This makes blockchain a very secure way to keep track of transactions. With cryptocurrency, you can send and receive payments directly without needing a bank, and all transactions are secure and can't be changed once they're made. Transactions with cryptocurrencies like Bitcoin, Ethereum, or even those quirky Dogecoins are recorded on this blockchain, ensuring that they are secure and, once made, irreversible.

What really makes cryptocurrencies stand out in the crowded playground of financial options? It's their ability to cut out the middleman—no banks, no fees for transferring money, no waiting periods. It's like sending an email; you send your crypto directly to someone else, and—BOOM!—transaction completed. This simplicity and speed, combined with the allure of sometimes making hefty profits, have catapulted cryptocurrencies from a geeky niche to a significant player in the digital age economy.

Risks and Rewards: The Crypto Roller Coaster

Now, hold on to your hats because if you thought roller coasters at the amusement park were a thrill, the cryptocurrency market takes it to a new level. Prices can skyrocket, then plunge to knee-shaking lows, all within the time it takes to binge-watch your favorite series. The reasons? Everything from changes in market sentiment, technological advancements, regulatory news, or even tweets from high-profile individuals can sway prices dramatically.

The rewards can be tempting—stories of crypto millionaires who timed their investments right are enough to make anyone's ears perk up. However, for every success story, there are tales of those who faced significant losses. It's crucial to remember that investing in crypto should be more about strategy and less about following the hype. Think of it as a spice in your investment stew—not the main ingredient, but something you add thoughtfully to enhance your overall portfolio.

Safe Practices: Keeping Your Digital Wallet Secure

If you're ready to dip your toes in the crypto waters, how do you keep your investment safe? First, think about storage. Cryptocurrencies are stored in digital wallets, which can be online, on your computer, or even on a hardware device, almost resembling a USB drive. Each type has its pros and cons regarding security and ease of use. Online wallets are convenient but vulnerable to hacking. Hardware wallets, while less convenient for quick trading, offer an extra layer of security by keeping your crypto offline.

Next, consider the platforms you use for buying and trading crypto. Not all platforms are created equal. Look for ones with strong security measures, positive user reviews, and transparency. Ensure that they use two-factor authentication, which adds an additional layer of security beyond just a password. Always ensure you have strong, unique passwords for your accounts. It's like locking your car—taking a few extra seconds to ensure security can save a lot of headaches later.

Regulatory and Tax Implications: Navigating the Crypto Legal Landscape

Just because crypto operates independently of traditional banks doesn't mean it's a free-for-all. Governments are increasingly interested in regulating cryptocurrencies, which can impact their value, how they're traded, and what you need to report come tax time. Staying informed about the regulatory environment in your country is crucial. For instance, in the U.S., the IRS treats cryptocurrencies as property, not currency, meaning gains or losses from crypto transactions are subject to capital gains tax.

When it comes to taxes, it's essential to keep detailed records of your transactions, including dates, amounts, and what the transaction was for. This documentation will be invaluable when reporting your taxes and ensuring that you're compliant with the laws. Remember that the anonymity of crypto transactions doesn't mean they're invisible to tax authorities. As with any investment, being upfront and transparent is your best policy.

Navigating the world of cryptocurrencies can be as exciting as it is bewildering. With their potential for high returns comes a not-insignificant level of risk and a steep learning curve. By understanding the basics, being aware of the risks, practicing secure investing habits, and staying informed about regulatory changes, you can better prepare yourself to make educated decisions in the crypto market. Whether you decide to invest or not, understanding this evolving landscape is becoming increasingly important in our digital world, offering insights into the future of your money but into the future of global finance itself.

5.5 RETIREMENT ACCOUNTS: NOT JUST FOR ADULTS

So, you think retirement is just for old folks? Think again! Starting to stash away some cash for your golden years while you're still in your golden youth can be one of the savviest financial moves you make. Why? One word: compounding. This magical finance wizardry allows your savings to grow exponentially over time as you earn interest on your interest. Think of it this way: the earlier you plant a tree, the longer it has to grow tall and strong.

Now, let's chat about the types of retirement accounts that can help you grow that mighty oak. There are IRAs (Individual Retirement Accounts) and employer-sponsored plans like 401(k)s. Choosing between them is a bit like picking your favorite ice cream flavor— each has its perks.

Traditional IRAs are like classic vanilla; you get tax deductions on your contributions now, which means you can lower your taxable income today, but you'll pay taxes when you withdraw the money in retirement. Roth IRAs? They're more like a reverse chocolate sundae; you pay taxes on your contributions now, but when you retire, you can make withdrawals tax-free. Sweet, right?

Then there's the 401(k), often offered through employers, which can feel like getting a double scoop. You contribute pre-tax income (lowering your taxable income now), and many employers will match a portion of your contributions. It's like getting free toppings on your sundae because who doesn't love free stuff? However, with 401(k)s, you'll pay taxes when you withdraw the money during retirement.

Navigating the limits and benefits of these accounts is essential. For 2024, you can contribute up to $6,500 a year to IRAs if you're under 50, and up to $22,500 a year to 401(K)s. These caps occasionally grow to account for inflation, like how your jeans might feel a bit tighter after Thanksgiving dinner, so you adjust the waistband. Staying within these limits while maximizing contributions can significantly impact the size of your retirement fund. Think of it as playing a financial Tetris; the better you fit your pieces within the limits, the clearer your path to a solid financial future.

Now, let's go on to automating your contributions because, let's be honest, remembering to transfer money every month is a hassle. Setting up an automatic transfer from your paycheck to your retirement account ensures that you consistently save without even thinking about it. Plus, it removes the temptation to spend what you might otherwise save. Out of sight, out of mind, right into your future pockets.

At 20, Emma decided to secure her financial future by opening a Roth IRA. Despite a modest income from her part-time job, she committed to contributing $200 a month, setting up automatic transfers to stay on track. She chose low-fee index funds for a diversified portfolio.

By starting early, Emma capitalized on compound interest. Contributing $200 monthly with an average annual return of 7%, she is projected to grow her savings to over $500,000 by age 60, from just $96,000 in contributions.

At 30, Mike decided to start saving for retirement. With a stable income, he committed to contributing $500 a month to a Roth IRA, setting up automatic transfers to stay disciplined. He chose low-fee index funds for a diversified portfolio. Starting later, Mike will miss out on some compound interest benefits. Contributing $500 monthly, with an average annual return of 7%, he is projected to grow his savings to over $400,000 by age 60, from $180,000 in contributions.

See the difference 10 years can make? Emma contributed $84,000 less than Mike, but her savings will grow to be over $100,000 more. Her early and disciplined approach to saving highlights the power of starting young and being consistent.

As we wrap up this chapter on the ins and outs of investing, from micro-investing to retirement planning, remember that investing is not just about growing your wealth. It's about creating opportunities for yourself and ensuring a secure and fulfilling future. Whether you're trading stocks, saving up in ETFs, or planning for retirement, each step builds greater financial independence.

ACTION CHECKLIST FOR BEGINNERS IN INVESTING

1. Start with Micro-Investing

- Choose a Micro-Investing Platform: Find one with low fees and user-friendly features.
- Set Up Automatic Round-Ups: Enable round-up features to invest spare change from everyday purchases.
- Start Small: Begin with small amounts to build the habit of investing.

2. Automate Your Investments

- Set Up Automatic Transfers: Arrange for regular transfers to your investment account (weekly, biweekly, or monthly).
- Use Dollar-Cost Averaging: Invest a fixed amount at regular intervals to mitigate market volatility.

3. Understand Risk and Return

- **Assess Your Risk Tolerance**: Determine how much risk you can handle based on your financial goals.
- **Diversify Your Investments**: Spread your money across different assets to minimize risk.

4. Set Clear Investment Goals

- Define Short-Term and Long-Term Goals: Identify what you're investing for and the timeline.
- Align Investments with Goals: Choose investments that match your risk tolerance and timeline for each goal.

5. Educate Yourself on Different Investment Types

- Learn About Bonds: Understand their role as stable, interest-earning investments.
- Explore Mutual Funds and ETFs: Consider these for diversification and professional management.
- Understand the Stock Market: Learn how to read stock charts and the importance of diversification.

6. Stay Consistent and Patient

- Regularly Review Your Portfolio: Monitor your investments and make adjustments as needed.
- Stick to Your Plan: Keep investing regularly, regardless of market conditions.

7. Secure Your Investments

- Use Secure Platforms: Ensure that your investment platform has strong security measures.
- Keep Records: Maintain detailed records of your investments for tax purposes.

CHAPTER 6
EARNING MORE

Never spend money before you have earned it.

THOMAS JEFFERSON

Managing the money you have is crucial, but increasing your earnings can go a long way as you strive to attain true financial independence. This chapter will guide you through practical strategies to boost your income, from landing your first job to navigating the gig economy and turning hobbies into profitable ventures. By applying these techniques, you can achieve financial stability and pave the way for future success. Whether you're just starting out or looking to diversify your income streams, this chapter offers actionable insights to help you earn more and reach your financial goals.

6.1 PROVEN TECHNIQUES FOR JOB HUNTING SUCCESS: A PRACTICAL GUIDE

Finding employment as a teen or young adult can be an exciting yet challenging experience. It's an important and necessary part of growing into the next phase of life, but it takes some effort on your part. Start by crafting a solid resume—consider it your personal highlight reel. Even if you don't have much work experience, you can spotlight volunteer work, school projects, and extracurricular activities. Skills like teamwork, communication, and problem-solving are your star players here. Keep your resume concise, professional, and tailored to each job you're applying for.

Next up is networking. Don't underestimate the power of personal connections. Talk to family, friends, teachers, and community members about your job search. They might know about hidden job opportunities that aren't listed online. Volunteering and internships are also excellent ways to build your network and gain valuable experience that can lead to job offers.

Preparing for interviews is another important step. Practice answering common interview questions and developing clear, concise responses highlighting your skills and experiences. Dress the part, show up on time, and bring your A-game with positive body language and good communication skills. Think of it like playing a role in a performance—posture, eye contact, and active listening are key to making a great impression.

Being proactive and persistent is also vital. Apply to multiple job listings, and follow up with employers after you submit your applications. Showing genuine interest and enthusiasm can set you apart from the crowd. Explore various types of employment, such as part-time jobs, seasonal work, and freelance opportunities. These positions can provide valuable experience and help you build a solid work ethic.

Finally, never stop learning. Take advantage of online courses, workshops, and certifications related to your field of interest. Continuous learning shows potential employers that you're dedicated and eager to grow. By following these best practices, teens and young adults can boost their chances of landing meaningful employment and can lay the groundwork for a successful career.

Of course, everyone dreams of having a fulfilling job that they love, but this phase of life is the time to get experience, pay your bills, and focus on gaining the education or career training needed to reach your future goals. You might not love your job today, but it's a stepping stone to help you build the skills and financial stability needed for tomorrow's opportunities. Embrace this phase as a necessary part of your journey, knowing that each experience brings you closer to your desired career and life.

The Impact of Social Media on Your Future

In today's digital age, your social media presence is more than just a way to connect with friends and share your experiences; it's also a window into your character for prospective employers, landlords, admissions committees, and others. These individuals often look at your social media profiles to get a sense of who you are beyond your resume or application. This practice can significantly impact your opportunities, so it's essential to manage your online presence carefully.

Employers use social media to screen candidates before making hiring decisions. They look for red flags such as inappropriate content, discriminatory comments, or any behavior that might suggest a lack of professionalism. Posts that show poor judgment, such as excessive partying or illegal activities, can make employers question your reliability and integrity. On the other hand, positive posts about volunteer work, academic achievements, and other constructive activities can enhance your appeal, showing that you are responsible and well-rounded.

Landlords also use social media to evaluate potential tenants. They are looking for responsible individuals who will take care of their property and be good neighbors. It's important to present yourself as someone who respects others and maintains a stable lifestyle.

College admissions officers often check applicants' profiles to gain insights into their character, leadership, and extracurricular activities. Internship coordinators look for professionalism and alignment with company culture. Volunteer organizations ensure potential volunteers align with their mission and values. Loan officers and financial institutions may assess an applicant's stability and reliability through their online presence. Professional licensing boards review social media to ensure candidates meet ethical and professional standards. Athletic programs and professional sports teams scrutinize profiles to evaluate behavior, attitude, and suitability for the team's culture. Government agencies, especially for security clearances or government jobs, conduct thorough social media reviews to assess an individual's reliability and trustworthiness.

By being aware of who might be viewing your social media, you can take steps to present yourself in a positive and professional light, enhancing your chances of success in various applications.

6.2 THE GIG ECONOMY AND YOU: OPPORTUNITIES AND RISKS

Fortunately, there are more ways than ever to earn money in today's world, and the gig economy might just be the sidekick your wallet needs. The gig economy is a vibrant universe where short-term tasks, freelance assignments, and temporary contracts thrive. It's like the Wild West of the job market, offering freedom, flexibility, and a fistful of dollars for those ready to hustle.

Understanding the Gig Economy: More Than Just a Buzzword

So, what's the gig economy really about? Imagine a marketplace buzzing like a downtown bazaar, where skills meet opportunities in a flurry of transactions. This economic model is fueled by freelance jobs, project-based work, and temporary contracts—think driving for Uber, designing graphics on a per-project basis, or coding up a storm for a startup over a weekend. What makes the gig economy tick is its flexibility; it allows you to work when you want, how you want, and as much as you want. It's tailored for the Netflix generation—on-demand and highly personalized.

Finding Gig Work: Your Gateway to Flexibility

Ready to dive in? Finding gig work that suits your skills can be as exciting as shopping for those perfect, not-too-tight, not-too-baggy jeans. Start by taking inventory of what you can do and what you enjoy. Can you write catchy content, design sleek websites, or capture stunning photos? Platforms like *Upwork*, *Fiverr*, and *TaskRabbit* are the shopping malls for gig work, where you can pick and choose opportunities that fit your style. Set up a profile, showcase your skills, and browse the gigs. It's like online dating, but instead of finding your soul mate, you match with the perfect job.

Exploring Online Platforms: The Digital Storefronts

Platforms such as *Upwork*, *Fiverr*, and *Etsy* serve as your launchpad. They're similar to those trendy pop-up stores in the city, except that they pop up right on your screen. *Upwork* is great for a wide range of freelance work—from writing and graphic design to web development and marketing. *Fiverr* offers gigs that start at $5 (hence the name), perfect for smaller tasks or building up your portfolio. *Etsy* is the go-to for selling anything handcrafted—from knitted scarves to hand-painted mugs. These platforms connect you to clients and handle the payment and feedback details, letting you focus on what you do best.

Building a Strong Profile: Your Digital Handshake

Think of your online profile as your professional handshake—strong, confident, and promising quality. Here's the twist: you're not there in person, so your profile needs to sing your praises for you. Start with a professional photo—yes, ditch the beach selfie. Write a clear, concise description of your skills and what you bring to the table. Include a portfolio of your best work—your personal highlight reel. Customer reviews can be pure gold. Encourage clients to leave feedback—it's word-of-mouth for the digital age.

Networking and Building Relationships: Beyond the Screen

While the gig economy might seem like a solo journey, it's really a bustling network of professionals just like you. Building relationships is important. Connect with other freelancers, join online forums, and participate in community discussions. Platforms like LinkedIn can be great for this. It's like mingling at a party, except everyone's potentially your next client or collaborator. The stronger your network, the more likely you are to land gigs regularly.

Managing Gig Income: Not Just Pocket Change

Here comes the tricky part—managing your gig income. Unlike a steady paycheck, gig work can fluctuate, making budgeting feel like a game of whack-a-mole. First, track all of your income and expenses diligently. Consider setting aside a portion of each gig payment for taxes (yes, Uncle Sam will want a piece of your pie). Here's a pro tip: funnel some of your earnings into an emergency fund. It's your financial backup plan, providing a cushion for slower months.

Navigating Risks: The Safety Nets

The gig economy isn't without its pitfalls. Job insecurity and the lack of benefits—like health insurance or a retirement plan—are real concerns. Mitigate these risks by diversifying your gig sources so all your income eggs aren't in one basket. Look into freelance unions or groups that offer member benefits, including health insurance. Always read the fine print on gig contracts to know what you're getting into and protect your rights.

Navigating the gig economy is like mastering a new game. The rules are different, the pace is faster, and the rewards—while potentially greater—come with their own set of challenges. Even so, with a bit of savvy, a dash of caution, and a whole lot of hustle, the gig economy can not just supplement your income but might even revamp your career. Just remember, in this game, flexibility is your best friend, and your ability to adapt is your ace in the hole. Ready to play?

6.3 FROM PASSION TO PROFIT: TURNING HOBBIES INTO CASH

Imagine that your weekend dabbling in painting, coding, or even gardening could actually fatten your wallet. Transforming hobbies into a source of income is not just for the lucky few; it's a real possibility for anyone willing to channel their passion into profit. The secret sauce? Recognizing which of your hobbies has market potential and understanding how to monetize it effectively.

First up, identify your marketable hobbies. Consider what you love doing so much that you lose track of time—maybe it's creating digital art, baking cupcakes, or making handmade jewelry. Now, ask yourself, "Would someone pay for this?" If you often get compliments or requests from friends or family for your creations, that's a green light. Dive deeper by researching online. Check out forums, social media, and marketplaces to see if there's a demand for your hobby. For instance, if you're into knitting, a quick search on *Etsy* or *Pinterest* can reveal how much people are willing to pay for hand-knitted scarves or beanies. You want to find a niche that both excites you and appeals to potential customers.

Now, where to showcase your newfound business? The platform you choose can make a big difference. If your hobby involves creating tangible goods like artwork or crafts, *Etsy* is great for selling handmade items. It's user-friendly and boasts a large audience specifically looking for unique, handcrafted products. For digital services like graphic design or video editing, platforms like YouTube can be a medium to showcase your skills and earn through ad revenue and sponsorships. Let's not forget about Instagram, which is perfect for visually-oriented hobbies like photography or food art. It provides a global stage to display your work and to attract customers through engaging posts and stories.

Pricing your work can be as tricky as being a cat on a skateboard. You need to find that sweet spot where customers feel they're getting value and you feel fairly compensated for your time and skill. Start by researching what others in the market charge for similar products or services. Don't just go with the lowest price— consider the quality and uniqueness of what you offer. A good strategy is to calculate your costs (materials, time, overhead) and add a profit margin that feels right. Remember that you must cover costs while valuing your creativity and effort.

Marketing doesn't have to mean putting on a suit and playing buzz-word bingo. At its core, it's about connecting with people who might love your work. Start by telling your story. Why do you create what you do? What's special about it? Use your social media platforms to share these stories, along with high-quality images or videos of your products or behind-the-scenes peeks into your creative process. Engage with your followers by responding to comments, asking questions, and even running small contests. This builds a community around your brand, turning casual viewers into loyal customers.

Customer engagement is the cherry on top. Making a sale is great, but you also want to create an experience that keeps people coming back. Include personalized thank-you notes in your orders, offer special discounts to repeat customers, or keep them updated with exciting developments through newsletters. When customers feel valued, they're not only more likely to buy again but also to spread the word. In today's digital age, a happy customer can be your best marketing tool, sharing their positive experiences and thus drawing a broader audience to your offerings.

By transforming your hobby into a profitable venture, you're earning extra cash and enriching your life by doing what you love. It's about leveraging your natural talents and passions, turning them into an enterprise that brings joy not just to you but also to your customers. So, take that hobby off the back burner and turn it into something amazing, one step at a time.

6.4 BALANCING SIDE HUSTLES WITH SCHOOL AND/OR WORK

Imagine you're a circus juggler, but instead of colorful balls, you're keeping school, a job, and a side hustle in the air. Here's the twist —none of those balls can afford to drop. This is the reality for many hustlers who are grinding to make ends meet, save for a dream, or fund their next big adventure. Balancing this trifecta requires some serious skills in time management, boundary setting, productivity, and a clear-eyed view of what each gig really adds to your life.

Let's kick off with time management, your secret weapon in the war against the clock. Effective time management is about prioritizing and giving each aspect of your life its due without burning the midnight oil too often. Start with the basics: get yourself a planner or use a digital calendar. Block out times for school, work, and side hustles, but also carve out time for rest, exercise, and a bit of fun. Create a rhythm that keeps you engaged but not overwhelmed. Check out systems like the Pomodoro Technique, in which you work in focused bursts followed by short breaks, which can dramatically increase your productivity without leading to burnout. Remember that the goal is to run a marathon, not a sprint—your pace needs to sustain you long-term.

Now, on to setting boundaries—your defense mechanism against the world's demands. It's easy to say yes to every project, every shift, or every request, but at what cost? Setting clear boundaries involves knowing when to say no, and that's a powerful skill. It recognizes when a gig is pulling too much from your energy reserves and threatens to tip your work-life balance into the red. Communicate your availability clearly to your employers or clients, stick to it, and guard your off-time zealously. Respect your own limits and ensure that others do the same. Your time and energy aren't infinite resources, and managing them wisely sometimes means guarding the gates.

Maximizing productivity is where you get to shine. Work smarter, not harder. Tools and apps can be lifesavers here. Use task management apps like *Asana* or *Trello* to keep track of your projects and deadlines. Automate where possible—set up email filters, use accounting software to track gig earnings, or schedule social media posts using tools like *Buffer*. Each little efficiency adds up, freeing you to focus on the work itself rather than on the administration of the work. Additionally, create a conducive work environment. A dedicated workspace, whether it's a desk in your bedroom or a spot at the local café, can signal to your brain that it's time to focus, increasing your output and decreasing the time it takes to get your tasks done.

Finally, evaluating the worth of your side hustle is crucial. Not all gigs are created equal. Some might offer more money; others might offer more satisfaction or skill-building opportunities. Regularly assess whether your side hustles align with your financial goals and personal values. Are they worth the time and energy you're investing? If a hustle isn't meeting your expectations, it might be time to reconsider or replace it. This evaluation isn't only about monetary gain; it's about ensuring that your side hustles enrich your life, not detract from it.

Managing the balancing act of school, work, and side hustles is no small feat. It requires a clear strategy, disciplined time management, firm boundaries, and constant evaluation to ensure alignment with your goals. As you move forward, keep these tools in your arsenal, and you'll not only survive the juggling act but also thrive, making each component of your busy life work for you, not against you.

As we wrap up this chapter on maximizing your earning potential through side hustles, remember the key takeaways: manage your time like a pro, set and respect your boundaries to avoid burnout, boost your productivity with smart tools and habits, and regularly evaluate the contribution of your side gigs to your financial and personal growth. These strategies will ensure that your side hustles are a beneficial addition to your life, complementing your main commitments and helping you build toward your goals.

ACTION STEPS FOR EARNING MORE

1. Create a Strong Resume:

- Highlight volunteer work, school projects, and key skills.
- Keep it concise and tailored to each job.

2. Network Effectively:

- Use personal connections and internships to find job opportunities.

3. Prepare for Interviews:

- Practice common questions, and use positive body language.

4. Explore the Gig Economy:

- Use platforms like *Upwork*, *Fiverr*, and *TaskRabbit* to find freelance work.
- Build a strong online profile and manage gig income responsibly.

5. Turn Hobbies into Cash:

- Identify marketable hobbies and use platforms like *Etsy* and Instagram to sell.
- Engage customers with personalized touches and good marketing.

CHAPTER 7
TAXES 101

In this world, nothing can be said to be certain, except death and taxes.

BENJAMIN FRANKLIN

I magine that it's payday and you're ready to buy all of your essentials, add to your emergency fund and have a little bit of fun, but when you get your hands on your paycheck, the numbers seem to have played a cruel game of shrinkage. Where did all that money go? And who is FICA? Welcome to the world of taxes and withholdings, the villains of your paycheck drama. Let's look at that pay stub, decode those deductions, and maybe even find a way to keep a bit more of your money when the next payday rolls around.

7.1 UNDERSTANDING YOUR PAYCHECK: TAXES EXPLAINED

Deciphering Your Pay Stub: Breaking Down the Various Deductions and What They Mean

First up is that pay stub. At first glance, you'll see your gross income, which is your salary, before any deductions or taxes. Then comes the not-so-fun part—deductions. These might include federal and state taxes, Social Security, Medicare, and possibly a slew of others, depending on where you live and work. Each deduction takes a piece of your paycheck before it hits your bank account.

First up is a payroll tax called FICA (Federal Insurance Contributions Act), which is used to fund Social Security and Medicare. It is pretty straightforward: they fund your future self's retirement days and medical needs. But federal and state taxes? They're like a subscription fee for living and working in your country and state— they pay for roads, schools, emergency services, and more. Your pay stub likely shows both the amount taken out for this pay period and the total for the year, which can be helpful come tax time or for financial planning.

Federal vs. State Taxes

On to the battle of the taxes: federal vs. state. Everyone pays federal taxes, which go into the nation's big money pot to fund nationwide programs and services. But state taxes? They're the wildcard. Depending on where you live, you might pay high state taxes, no state taxes, or something in between. States like Texas and Florida boast a no-state-income-tax policy, giving residents a bit more leeway in their personal budgets. Others, like California and New York, take a more significant bite. Understanding this can dramatically affect your take-home pay and might even influence future decisions about where you live and work.

Common Tax Terms Explained

We've touched on gross income—your salary before all the deductions, but what about net income? That's your take-home pay after all those hungry little deductions have had their fill. If gross income is your pie in the sky, net income is the pie you actually get to eat. Withholdings are how much of your pie is set aside for taxes during each pay period. It's a forced savings account for your tax bill; saving gradually is better than being hit with a huge bill at once.

Adjusting Your Withholdings: How to Ensure You're Not Overpaying or Underpaying Taxes Throughout the Year

Speaking of withholdings, did you know you can adjust these? If you typically get a huge tax refund, you might be overdoing it on withholdings, giving the government a free loan from your paycheck. Conversely, if you end up owing a lot at tax time, you might need to withhold more. Adjusting your withholdings can help keep your paycheck and tax liabilities in balance. It's like tuning your guitar to make sure it's pitch-perfect for your next concert—get the withholdings right, and your financial tune sounds sweet all year long.

Changing the tax withholdings from your paycheck typically involves updating your tax withholdings form(s) with your employer. Here are the general steps you can follow:

1. Obtain the Correct Form(s): In the U.S., this is the IRS Form W-4. Other countries may have similar forms for adjusting federal tax withholdings. In the U.S., there may also be a parallel form for your state.

2. Fill Out the Form:

- **Personal Information**: Provide your name, address, Social Security number, and marital status.
- **Multiple Jobs**: If you have more than one job, you might need to account for additional withholding.
- **Other Adjustments**: You can specify other income, deductions, and extra withholding amounts as needed.

3. Submit the Form: Once filled out, submit the form to your employer's HR or payroll department. Some employers have an online system for updating your W-4 electronically.

4. Review Paychecks: After submitting the form, review your subsequent paychecks to ensure that the withholdings changes have been correctly implemented.

5. Re-evaluate Periodically: It's a good idea to re-evaluate your withholdings periodically, especially if you experience life changes or changes in income.

Refer to the form's instructions for detailed instructions, or consult a tax professional if you're unsure how to fill it out.

Navigating the intricacies of your paycheck and understanding where your money goes can empower you to make smarter financial decisions. We would all love to keep a bit more of that hard-earned cash to enjoy right now. Who knows? With a little tweaking, your emergency fund may get a little bigger, no magic required—just a better understanding of your taxes and withholdings.

7.2 FILING YOUR TAXES: A STEP-BY-STEP GUIDE

Preparation Is Key: The documents and information you need to gather before you start the filing process

Okay, so it's tax season again—the time of year when adulting hits hard and all that paperwork you've shoved in a drawer comes back to haunt you. But fear not! With a bit of prep, you can tackle your taxes like a boss. First things first. Let's talk about gathering your documents. This is like prepping for a big project. Having all your materials at hand makes the process way smoother. You'll need:

- W-2 forms from employers
- 1099 forms if you've done freelance work
- Interest statements from banks if you've got savings or investment accounts.
- Have you paid tuition or student loan interest? Grab those forms too (1098-E for student loan interest and 1098-T for tuition statements).
- If you've made any charitable donations, those receipts are golden for possible deductions.

Choosing the Right Filing Status: How to choose the one that gives you the best tax advantages

Now, let's navigate the maze of filing statuses. Your filing status is a key player in the tax game—it affects your filing requirements, standard deduction amounts, and eligibility for certain credits and deductions. The main statuses are Single, Married Filing Jointly, Married Filing Separately, Head of Household, and Qualifying Widow(er) with Dependent Child. Single is pretty straightforward—

if you're not married, this is likely you. Married Filing Jointly often results in lower taxes and higher deductions, but if you and your spouse prefer to keep your finances separate, or if one of you has significant medical expenses, filing separately might be the way to go. Head of Household is for unmarried folks who pay more than half the cost of keeping up a home for themselves and a qualifying person (like a child or parent). Lastly, if your spouse has passed away and you have a dependent child, you might qualify as a Qualifying Widow(er), which allows you to use joint return tax rates and the highest standard deduction for up to two years after the death. Choose wisely; the right status can significantly impact your tax situation.

Navigating Tax Forms: The most common tax forms, such as the W-2, 1099, and 1040

Feeling overwhelmed by tax forms? Let's take a look at the main characters in this drama. The W-2 form is pretty much your employment summary—how much you earned and what was taken out for taxes. It's your financial report card from your employer. Then there's the 1099 form, the freelancers' companion—it reports income from freelance work, dividends, or interest. Now, the star of the show: the 1040 form. This is where you summarize your entire year—income, deductions, credits—and finally, get to see how much you owe or get back. It's like the final exam, where you show your work and figure out your grade (in this case, your tax refund or liability).

Filing Methods: Pros and cons of different filing methods

When it comes to filing your taxes, you've got options. Old school paper filing is like handwriting your term paper—it's reliable, but it can be slow, and the risk of mistakes is higher. Enter tax software, the modern solution that's like using a word processor with spell check

—it makes everything easier and faster, often with step-by-step guidance and calculations that reduce errors. Additionally, e-filing through software generally means a quicker refund. But what if your tax situation is complex, or you just really don't want to deal with it? That's when a tax professional comes in handy. Think of them as a tutor who can help you navigate complex problems and ensure that everything is correct. Sure, it costs more, but for peace of mind and potentially maximized deductions, it can be well worth it.

Common Filing Mistakes: Common errors to avoid when filing your taxes

Finally, let's talk about common pitfalls. Common mistakes include incorrect social security numbers, forgetting to sign your return or missing deadlines—all of which can lead to delays or penalties. Double-check every entry, especially your personal info. Another biggie is not reporting all your income. Remember those 1099s? Yeah, the IRS (Internal Revenue Service) gets copies, too, so make sure everything matches up. Don't forget that deductions and credits are like bonus points that can lower your tax bill. Just make sure you have records to back them up because if the IRS calls you out, you'll need to show your work.

The IRS enforces tax laws by conducting audits (detailed examinations of individual tax returns to ensure accuracy and compliance with tax laws), investigating tax fraud and evasion, assessing penalties and interest on unpaid taxes, and taking legal action such as liens and levies to collect outstanding tax debts. A tax lien is when the government places a legal claim on your property because you didn't pay your taxes. The government can take your stuff, like your car or house, if you don't pay what you owe. A tax levy is a legal action to seize a taxpayer's assets to satisfy unpaid tax debts. This can include taking money directly from your bank account or "garnishing wages," which means the government can take money from your paycheck before you even get your hands on it. In short, always be accurate and honest with your taxes because the IRS will eventually find you if you don't, and it won't be a pleasant experience.

7.3 TAX DEDUCTIONS AND CREDITS FOR YOUNG ADULTS

Let's dive into tax deductions and credits, shall we? Think of these as the cheat codes of the tax world—they can seriously level up your tax return game, reducing how much you owe or boosting that sweet refund. First, a quick breakdown: deductions lower your taxable income (that's the amount of your income that's subject to taxes), while credits give you a dollar-for-dollar reduction on your actual tax bill. So, if deductions are like getting a discount when you buy a space rocket (because who doesn't dream a bit big?), credits are more like getting a rebate check after you've bought it.

Now, onto some gold nuggets you might not know about, specifically tailored for you, the young adults stepping into this fiscal jungle. We'll start with education expenses and student loan interest since education costs more than just a few pretty pennies these days. If you're currently paying off student loans, the IRS might be kinder than you think. You could deduct up to $2,500 of the interest you paid on your student loans over the year. Yes, that's money you can subtract directly from your taxable income, which might help take the sting out of those monthly payments. Just remember that there are income limits that might phase out this deduction, so if you've landed a particularly lucrative gig, double-check to see if you still qualify.

There's more on the education front. Credits like the American Opportunity Credit (AOC) can be a game-changer. This gem offers up to $2,500 per student per year for the first four years of college.

Expenses that count toward this credit aren't just tuition; they also include books, supplies, and equipment. However, there's a plot twist—40% of it is refundable, which means if the credit drops your tax liability to zero, you could get up to $1,000 back. Let's not forget its cousin, the Lifetime Learning Credit, which offers up to $2,000 per tax return (not per student) and doesn't require a minimum course load, making it perfect if you're taking career development classes or pursuing graduate studies part-time.

Maximizing these deductions and credits involves a bit of strategy. First, keep impeccable records. Every form, receipt, or document related to educational expenses should be filed and ready to whip out if needed. Don't just shove them in a shoebox under your bed. Organize them in a way that would make Marie Kondo proud. Next, if you're juggling school and a side hustle, make sure to explore every possible credit or deduction related to both. Sometimes, educational expenses can overlap with business expenses, especially if your studies directly relate to your business. This overlap can sometimes offer double the deductions if navigated correctly.

Navigating the nuances of these tax benefits might seem daunting, but understanding them can lead to significant savings. Armed with this knowledge, you can approach your taxes with a newfound confidence, ready to claim every credit and deduction you rightfully deserve. With each tax season, you'll get better at spotting and maximizing these opportunities, turning what was once a bewildering chore into a rewarding annual ritual. So, gear up, get your documents in order, and remember: in the game of taxes, knowledge is not just power—it's money.

7.4 GIG WORK AND TAXES: WHAT YOU NEED TO KNOW

Let's face it: the gig economy isn't just a buzzword—it's your late-night Uber rides, your weekend photo shoots, and those graphic design gigs that keep your creativity buzzing. But when it comes to taxes, gig work can feel like stepping onto a roller coaster that's missing a few crucial signs. Are you strapped in and ready? Let's look at the tax maze that every gig worker needs to navigate.

Self-Employment Tax Responsibilities: Navigating the Waters of Gig Economy Taxes

First up are self-employment taxes. If you've ever wondered why your musician friend keeps mumbling about self-employment taxes, here's the scoop. When you work a regular 9-to-5, your employer handles your Social Security and Medicare taxes, neatly deducting them from your paycheck. However, in the realm of gig work, you are the boss, and the taxman expects you to handle this on your own. This means paying both the employee's and the employer's share of Social Security and Medicare, which totals up to approximately 15.3% of your net earnings. Sounds hefty, right? It's like finding out your free streaming service trial has ended, and now you've got to pay up if you want to keep binge-watching.

Now, to prevent an end-of-year tax horror show, the IRS wants its cut quarterly. That's right; quarterly estimated tax payments are your new season tickets to the gig worker's tax game. Mark your calendar for mid-April, June, September, and January. Missing these dates can lead to penalties, kind of like racking up late fees at a library, except these books cost a lot more. To figure out how much to pay, you'll need to estimate your yearly earnings and calculate the corresponding taxes. It's a bit like trying to guess how many jellybeans are in a jar.

Get it close, and you're golden. Way off? You might either owe a lump sum at tax time or get a refund.

Tracking Expenses: The Art of Keeping Meticulous Records

On to tracking expenses, which is less about hoarding every receipt and more about strategic saving. Every mile you drive, every lens you buy, and every cup of tea you sip while sketching out client designs could save you money on taxes. Why? Because these can be deductible expenses. To make sure you can take full advantage of deductible expenses, keep a detailed log of your income and expenses. Apps like *QuickBooks* or *Expensify* can turn this task into a breeze, categorizing your expenses and even tracking mileage through your phone's GPS. If you prefer a free method, just keep a folder handy and put your receipts in this folder throughout the year. Everything will be in one place and ready to go when tax time rolls around.

Here's a pro tip: not all expenses are created equal. Some are fully deductible, like advertising costs, while others, like meals, are only 50% deductible. Knowing the difference can be as crucial as knowing which wire to cut in a movie bomb-disposal scene—stressful, but with practice, you get better at making the right call.

As a teen or young adult working in the gig economy, there are several important tax deductions you can take advantage of to reduce your tax liability. Here are some key deductions to consider:

1. **Home office deduction**: If you use a portion of your home exclusively and regularly for your gig work, you can deduct a percentage of your rent, utilities, and other home-related expenses. To qualify, the space must be used solely for business purposes.
2. **Vehicle expenses:** If you use your car for gig work (e.g., rideshare driving), you can deduct either the actual

expenses or use the standard mileage rate. This includes costs like gas, insurance, and maintenance related to business use.

3. **Cell phone and internet:** You can deduct the portion of your cell phone bill and internet costs that are used for business purposes.

4. **Equipment and supplies:** Any equipment, tools, or supplies purchased specifically for your gig work are deductible. This could include laptops, printers, software subscriptions, or other job-specific items.

5. **Self-employment tax deduction:** You can deduct half of your self-employment tax, which covers Social Security and Medicare contributions.

6. **Health insurance premiums:** If you're self-employed and pay for your own health insurance, you may be able to deduct these premiums.

7. **Professional development:** Costs related to work-related education, training, or certifications can be deductible.

8. **Travel expenses:** If your gig work requires travel, you can deduct transportation, lodging, and meal costs (meals are typically 50% deductible, but were temporarily 100% deductible for 2021 and 2022).

9. **Advertising and marketing:** Expenses related to promoting your gig work, such as business cards or online ads, are deductible.

10. **Retirement contributions:** Contributions to self-employed retirement plans like SEP IRAs or Solo 401(k)s can be deductible.

It's crucial to keep detailed records of all your business-related expenses and income throughout the year. This will make it easier to claim deductions accurately when filing your taxes. Remember, you may need to make quarterly estimated tax payments to avoid penalties, as taxes are not automatically withheld from gig economy earnings.

Tax laws can change, and individual situations vary. It's always a good idea to consult with a qualified tax professional to ensure you're taking all the deductions you're entitled to and complying with tax regulations.

Form 1099-NEC: Understanding Your Gig Income Documentation

Enter Form 1099-NEC, the document that reports how much you've earned from each client who's paid you $600 or more during the year. No W-2s here—just a straightforward statement of what you've earned. What if a client ghosts you come tax season and doesn't send this form? First, don't panic. You should still report all your income, form or no form. Keep your own detailed records and invoices as proof of income because, unlike those mythical monsters under your bed, the IRS is very real and doesn't take kindly to unreported earnings.

Tax Tips for Gig Workers: Avoiding Common Pitfalls

Lastly, let's share some insider tax tips to keep you safe in the gig economy tax jungle. Always set aside a portion of each payment for taxes. Use a separate bank account for gig work to keep personal and professional finances distinct, which makes tracking and reporting much easier. Consider investing in a good accountant who understands self-employment nuances, especially if your gig work crosses into different tax categories or involves significant expenses.

Navigating taxes as a gig worker doesn't have to be a trip through a haunted house filled with surprises and scares. With the right tools, a bit of knowledge, and a proactive approach, you can turn this part of your gig life into a well-oiled machine—efficient, less terrifying, and maybe even rewarding. Keep your records straight, your estimates accurate, and your deadlines marked, and you'll master the art of gig economy taxes with the finesse of a seasoned pro.

7.5 SCHOLARSHIPS, GRANTS, AND TAXES: KEEPING IT STRAIGHT

Navigating the maze of scholarships and grants is like playing a game where the rules keep changing depending on whether you're using the funds for tuition or splurging on your dorm room pizza parties. Let's get this straight: not all scholarships and grants are created equal —at least, not in the eyes of the taxman. Generally, if you're using the money to pay for tuition, fees, books, and supplies directly required for your coursework, the IRS gives you a thumbs up—these aren't considered taxable income. However, if you use any part of that money for other expenses, like room and board or travel, it starts looking more like taxable income. Think of it as your scholarship going undercover—as long as it sticks to tuition and required supplies, it remains incognito from taxes.

Now, if you find yourself with scholarship or grant money that covers more than just the tuition costs, you'll need to report the extra as income. This often feels like discovering a plot twist in your favorite series—surprising, maybe a bit disappointing, but definitely something you need to handle. Reporting additional scholarship income is crucial because, just like any plot twist, ignoring it doesn't make it go away, and this could lead to complications later. When filing your tax return, this extra income needs to be included under the wages section, and yes, you'll need to pay taxes on it. It's like paying your dues for using that money on life's little extras outside your direct education costs.

Planning for Tax Implications: Strategize to Avoid End-of-Year Surprises

Planning for the tax implications of receiving scholarships or grants is like setting up chess pieces in a strategic game—the goal is to avoid checkmate when tax season rolls around. Start by understanding the full scope of how your scholarships or grants are allocated—how much is covering tuition and fees directly related to your coursework versus other expenses? Keeping detailed records throughout the year can save you a lot of headaches. Documentation is your ally, providing evidence if the IRS questions your tax return.

Moreover, consider how your scholarship impacts your eligibility for other tax credits and deductions. Sometimes, the tax benefits of declaring a portion of your scholarship as income (and thus paying taxes on it) might be outweighed by the larger deductions or credits you can claim. It's a balancing act, requiring a bit of math and maybe some professional advice to navigate effectively. Don't shy away from consulting a tax professional if things get complicated. They can help you get the best possible tax outcome.

Navigating the interplay among scholarships, grants, and taxes doesn't have to be a solo expedition fraught with uncertainty. With the right knowledge and strategies, you can manage your educational finances like a pro, maximizing benefits while staying compliant with tax laws. By understanding the tax implications of your scholarships and grants, and by making smart use of educational tax benefits, you're not just surviving the academic world; you're thriving financially within it.

Jane, a young graduate student balancing her studies with a part-time job, decided to learn about the intricacies of student tax credits to optimize her finances. By carefully documenting her tuition payments, textbook purchases, and school supplies, she was able to claim the American Opportunity Credit, which offered her up to $2,500 per year. Additionally, she deducted the interest on her student loans, reducing her taxable income further. This strategic use of tax credits and deductions not only minimized her tax liability but also resulted in a significant refund, easing the financial burden of her education and allowing her to save more for her future goals.

As this chapter closes, remember the importance of being proactive about your tax situation, especially when it comes to managing scholarships and grants. The knowledge you've gained here is more than just academic—it's a practical toolkit that will help you confidently navigate the complexities of taxes.

ACTION CHECKLIST FOR MANAGING YOUR TAXES

1. Understanding Your Paycheck: Taxes Explained

- Decipher Your Pay Stub: Understand the various deductions such as federal and state taxes, Social Security, and Medicare.
- Know the Difference: Differentiate between federal and state taxes and their impacts on your take-home pay.
- Familiarize Yourself with Terms: Learn key tax terms like gross income, net income, and withholdings.
- Adjust Withholdings: Use IRS Form W-4 to adjust your withholdings to avoid overpaying or underpaying taxes.

2. Filing Your Taxes: A Step-by-Step Guide

- Gather Documents: Collect necessary documents such as W-2s, 1099s, interest statements, and receipts for deductions.

- Choose Filing Status: Select the appropriate filing status (Single, Married Filing Jointly, etc.) for optimal tax advantages.
- Understand Common Tax Forms: Know the purposes of W-2, 1099, and 1040 forms.
- Decide on Filing Method: Choose between paper filing, tax software, or professional help based on your needs.
- Avoid Common Mistakes: Double-check entries, report all income, and meet deadlines to avoid penalties.

3. Tax Deductions and Credits for Young Adults

- Maximize Education Benefits: Utilize deductions for student loan interest, and credits like the American Opportunity Credit and the Lifetime Learning Credit.
- Keep Detailed Records: Maintain organized records of all educational expenses and related documents.
- Strategize Deductions: Explore overlapping deductions for education and business expenses if applicable.

4. Gig Work and Taxes: What You Need to Know

- Understand Self-Employment Taxes: Pay both the employee's and employer's share of Social Security and Medicare taxes.
- Make Quarterly Payments: Mark your calendar for quarterly estimated tax payments to avoid penalties.
- Track Expenses: Use apps or maintain logs to track income and deductible expenses meticulously.
- Report All Income: Ensure that all gig income is reported accurately, even if you don't receive a 1099 form.
- Set Aside Funds: Regularly set aside a portion of your income for tax payments to avoid year-end surprises.

5. Scholarships, Grants, and Taxes: Keeping It Straight

- Use Funds Appropriately: Understand that funds used for tuition and required supplies are non-taxable, while other uses may be taxable.
- Report Extra Income: Include any taxable portion of scholarships or grants in your income when filing taxes.
- Plan for Tax Implications: Keep detailed records and consider how scholarship funds impact your eligibility for other tax credits and deductions.

Additional Tips

- **Stay Organized**: Regularly update your records and documents to make tax time easier.
- **Consult Professionals**: Seek advice from tax professionals when dealing with complex tax situations.
- **Re-evaluate Periodically**: Review your tax situation periodically, especially after major life changes.

CHAPTER 8
PRACTICAL FINANCIAL PLANNING

Financial freedom is available to those who learn about it and work for it.

ROBERT KIYOSAKI

I magine that you're embarking on a road trip. You've got your snacks, playlist, and a vague notion that you're heading somewhere awesome. Wouldn't having a map, a clearly defined route, and some landmarks to visit along the way be better? That's what crafting a personalized financial roadmap is like. It's plotting your course in the financial universe, ensuring that each choice propels you toward your own version of success—be it buying your first car, owning a home, or maybe just ensuring that you can afford to be the life of the party without going broke.

8.1 CREATING A CUSTOMIZED FINANCIAL ROADMAP

Personalized Planning: Crafting Your Financial Future

Let's start with personalizing your financial plan. There isn't a cookie-cutter strategy that works for everyone. Aligning your financial strategy with your personal dreams, circumstances, and the quirky goals that make you, well, you, means your plan won't be the same as your peers. First, define what success looks like on your terms. Is it financial independence by 30? A tech startup? A travel fund that lets you explore the world? Once you have your goals in sight, you can set the GPS coordinates to your desired destination.

Now, think about your resources and limitations. Just as you can't drive a vintage scooter on a freeway at 100 mph, you need to assess your financial vehicle realistically. What's your income? What are your essential expenses? Understanding these helps you figure out how much fuel (read: money) you can divert toward your goals each month. Remember that this plan isn't static; it's a living document. Just as you might suddenly decide to detour to a cool, unplanned destination on a road trip, your financial plan should have the flexibility to adapt to life's unexpected turns.

Milestone Setting: Marking Your Financial Journey

Setting milestones within your financial roadmap is like planting flags on a mountain climb. Each flag marks a significant achievement, giving you a moment to celebrate and reassess. Let's say your goal is to save for a down payment on a house. Break this into smaller milestones. Your first milestone could be saving $1,000, then $5,000, and so on. These milestones keep you motivated and give you clear checkpoints to review your progress.

Adjusting Your Plan: Staying Agile on Your Financial Journey

John Lennon was onto something when he put this old saying into his lyrics, "Life is what happens when you're busy making other plans," the same goes for your financial roadmap. Maybe you land a higher-paying job, decide to go back to school, or face an unexpected financial hurdle. Your financial plan needs to be adjustable to accommodate these changes. Regular check-ins, like a yearly review or a sit-down every time a major life event happens, can help you tweak your roadmap. Maybe you divert more into savings because you've gotten a raise, or perhaps you scale back on investments to fund a return to college. The key is to keep your plan in sync with your life.

8.2 INSURANCE BASICS: WHAT YOU NEED AND WHY

Let's talk about insurance, but let's make it less yawn-inducing. Think of insurance like a trusty umbrella. You might not need it every day, but when an unexpected storm hits—like a sudden downpour of medical bills or car repairs—it's incredibly useful to have around. Most young adults can stay on their parent's insurance until they are 26 or out of college, but there will come a day when you will be on your own and need to take care of insurance like a real adult. Understanding insurance means recognizing that paying monthly premiums creates a safety net, allowing you to sleep soundly at night, secure in the knowledge that life's little (or big) surprises won't wipe you out financially.

Understanding the importance of insurance is like recognizing why you need to charge your phone—without power, it's just a fancy paperweight. Similarly, without insurance, you're one major accident or health issue away from a potential financial disaster. Insurance acts as a financial cushion, absorbing the impact of unexpected costs so you don't have to. By paying premiums, you transfer the risk of significant financial loss to the insurance company, which agrees to cover expenses for various surprise events, such as car accidents, theft, or medical emergencies.

Types of Insurance: Decoding What You Actually Need

Diving into the types of insurance is like walking into a buffet. There's a lot on offer, and while everything might look appealing, you need to pick what best suits your appetite—or, in this case, your needs. The big ones on the menu are health, auto, and renter's insurance. Health insurance is the broccoli of the insurance world—maybe not always exciting, but incredibly good for you. It covers your medical expenses, from doctor's visits to surgeries, and can help you manage the costs of both routine healthcare and unexpected medical issues. Without it, a single health emergency can become a financial disaster.

Then there's auto insurance, which is pretty much mandatory if you drive. It's your car's shield against the slings and arrows of outrageous fortune, like fender-benders or more serious accidents. It covers repairs to your vehicle and protects you against liability if you're at fault in an accident that causes injury or property damage to others.

Renter's insurance, on the other hand, might not be mandatory, but it's no less important, especially if you're fond of your electronics and belongings. It's a security blanket for your stuff. If your rental home is broken into, or if there's a fire or water damage, renter's insurance can help replace your belongings. Plus, it often includes liability coverage, which can be a lifesaver if someone is injured in your rental and decides to sue.

Shopping for Insurance: Finding the Best Fit Without Breaking the Bank

Shopping for insurance can be as tricky as online dating—what looks great at a quick glance might not be the perfect match for you. Comparing policies is key. Don't just look at the premiums; consider what's covered. A cheaper policy might save you money now but could cost you big time if it doesn't cover what you need when disaster strikes. Use online comparison tools to get a range of quotes, and read the fine print. Yes, it's tedious, but understanding exactly what you're covered for—and what you're not—can prevent a world of financial pain later on.

Also, check out reviews and ratings for insurance companies. How do they handle claims? Are customers satisfied with their service? An insurer's responsiveness and support when you're filing a claim can make a huge difference in your experience. It's like choosing a team-mate; you want someone reliable who will have your back in a tight spot.

Common Insurance Mistakes to Avoid: Sidestepping Potential Pitfalls

When it comes to insurance, some common blunders can end up costing you. Underinsuring is a classic—like buying rain boots that don't fit. Sure, you saved some money, but you'll get soaked when the storm hits. Always ensure your coverage limits are high enough to fully cover potential losses. On the flip side, there's over-insuring, which is like paying for a gourmet meal you'll never eat. Why shell out for coverage you realistically won't need?

Another frequent error is ignoring deductibles—the amount you pay out of pocket before your insurance kicks in. Opting for a low deductible might seem like a great idea until you see the higher monthly premiums. Sometimes, choosing a higher deductible makes sense if it significantly lowers your premiums and if you have enough savings to cover the deductible in an emergency.

Insurance and Risk Management: Fortifying Your Financial Fortress

In the grand scheme of things, having the right insurance policies is a critical part of managing financial risk. It's knowing your weak spots and fortifying them. Whether the situation is a medical issue, a car accident, or a burglar making off with your laptop, the right insurance can help keep an unfortunate incident from turning into a financial catastrophe. It allows you to plan for the unexpected, providing a safety net that lets you pursue your life and goals with one less worry hanging over your head.

As you navigate the complexities of adulting, give insurance its due consideration. It might not be the most thrilling part of your financial plan, but when life inevitably throws a curveball your way, you'll be glad you have that safety net ready and waiting. Just as a reliable tool is always ready when you need it, your insurance stands by quietly, ready to support you in times of need.

8.3 PLANNING FOR BIG PURCHASES: CARS, COLLEGE, AND MORE

Some of the most exciting chapters of your life involve hefty price tags—like buying your first car, venturing through college, or stepping into a home you can call your own. While these purchases can jazz up your life's soundtrack, they require more than just a spontaneous shopping spree.

Saving Strategies: Building Your Big-Purchase War Chest

First, let's talk about saving strategies. Big-ticket items aren't your everyday purchases; they're more like the boss levels in video games that require extra prep and strategy. Setting aside money for these big purchases should start as early as possible. This is where your savings snowball comes into play—you start small, but as it rolls down the hill, it picks up more snow, growing bigger, faster, and faster. Automate your savings if you can. Set up a separate savings account specifically for your goal, and funnel a portion of your income directly into it. This way, you're not tempted to spend what you can't see.

Consider high-yield savings accounts or certificates of deposit (CDs) for these goals. They offer higher interest rates, meaning your money grows faster without additional effort. If you're saving for something more than five years away, like a down payment on a house, you might even invest some of that money in low-risk bonds or mutual funds. The higher returns can significantly speed up your savings timeline, but remember that greater potential returns come with greater risk, so balance wisely.

Financing Options: Navigating the Seas of Loans and Payment Plans

Unless you've been secretly minting gold in your backyard, chances are you'll need some financing to help cover the costs of things like cars or college tuition. Here's where things can get tricky. Loans and payment plans are double-edged swords—they can cut through financial barriers, making your goals more accessible, but if handled carelessly, they can also hurt your financial health.

When considering loans, whether it's a student loan, mortgage, or car loan, scrutinize the terms. Look at the interest rates, repayment periods, and any penalties for early repayment. Fixed interest rates can offer predictability, preventing nasty surprises if rates go up in the future. However, if you anticipate that you might be able to pay off your debt early, make sure your loan doesn't have prepayment penalties that could eat into what you save on interest.

For college, explore federal student loans first, as they often have more favorable terms and repayment options compared to private loans. For cars and homes, good credit can be your best friend. It can snag you lower interest rates, significantly affecting how much you pay over time. Don't hesitate to shop around and negotiate terms. Sometimes, the sticker price isn't the final price, and this applies to loan conditions as well.

The Impact of Big Purchases on Financial Health: Keeping Your Balance

Big purchases can make or break your financial health. They're like adding heavy weights to your side of the financial seesaw. If not balanced correctly with the rest of your budget, they can leave you teetering on the edge of financial instability. Understanding how a big purchase fits into your overall financial picture is crucial. Will taking on a car payment mean you can't contribute to your retirement for a while? Will student loan repayments delay other financial goals, like buying a home? Mapping out your cash flow with these big purchases in mind can help you see where you might need to adjust your spending or increase your income to keep everything in harmony.

Practical Tips and Considerations: Mastering the Art of Big Purchases

Here are some practical tips. Research is your best tool when planning for a big purchase. Understand the market, know the average costs, and arm yourself with knowledge. For cars, know the best times to buy, like holiday sales, when dealerships are more likely to offer discounts. For homes, understand the local real estate market trends. Are home prices in your area going up or down? Is it a buyer's or a seller's market? For college, consider the return on investment of your chosen field of study. Will your expected future income justify the cost of your education?

Negotiating is another skill to hone. Whether it's the price of the car, the terms of a loan, or even financial aid for college, don't accept the first offer. Be polite, but be persistent. Often, there's room to maneuver that can work to your advantage.

Big purchases are more than just transactions. They're significant financial events that can have long-lasting impacts on your economic landscape. Like any major life decision, they require thought, planning, and a bit of savvy maneuvering. With the right strategies, you can ensure that these purchases enhance your life without derailing your financial goals.

As we wrap up this exploration into planning for big purchases, remember that each decision you make—from the savings plan you choose to the financing options you utilize to the negotiation strategies you employ—plays a crucial role in shaping your financial journey. These aren't just purchases; they're stepping stones to your future. Up next, we'll dive into the world of advanced investment strategies, where we'll explore how to further grow your wealth and secure your financial independence. Stay tuned because the path to financial mastery is just getting started.

ACTION STEPS FOR PRACTICAL FINANCIAL PLANNING

1. Creating a Customized Financial Roadmap

- Define Success: Identify your personal financial goals (e.g., financial independence, startup, travel fund).
- Assess Resources: Determine your income and essential expenses to understand your financial capacity.
- Set Milestones: Break down big goals into smaller, achievable targets (e.g., saving $1,000, then $5,000).
- Regular Reviews: Conduct periodic reviews to adjust your financial plan based on life changes or unexpected events.

2. Insurance Basics: What You Need and Why

- Understand Insurance Types: Know the essential kinds of insurance (health, auto, renter's) and their purposes.
- Shop Smart: Compare insurance policies, not just on premiums, but also on coverage and customer service.
- Avoid Common Mistakes: Ensure adequate coverage without over-insuring, and understand your deductible options.

3. Planning for Big Purchases: Cars, College, and More

- Start Saving Early: Set up separate savings accounts and automate deposits for big purchases.
- Consider High-Yield Accounts: Use high-yield savings accounts or CDs for faster growth of your savings.
- Evaluate Financing Options: Understand loan terms, interest rates, and repayment conditions before committing.

- Research and Negotiate: Thoroughly research the market and negotiate the best deals for your purchases.
- Impact on Financial Health: Assess how big purchases affect your overall financial situation and make necessary adjustments to maintain balance.

CHAPTER 9
PROTECTING YOUR FINANCIAL FUTURE

The best way to predict your future is to create it.

ABRAHAM LINCOLN

P icture this: you're on a roller coaster, strapped in, and about to plunge into a dizzying drop. Your heart races, your palms sweat, and a cocktail of excitement and fear bubbles up—it's thrilling, yet slightly terrifying. Now, imagine if your financial life felt like that all the time. Not so fun, right? That's what unchecked financial anxiety can do to you. It can turn your everyday money management into an emotional roller coaster that leaves you feeling drained. Let's talk about taming that ride, shall we?

9.1 NURTURING YOUR FINANCIAL MENTAL HEALTH

Understanding Financial Anxiety: Unmasking the Hidden Culprit

Financial anxiety sneaks up like a shadow, often disguising itself as fleeting worries about bills or distant thoughts of savings and retirement. But when it takes hold, it morphs into a constant presence, coloring your decisions and potentially leading to sleepless nights staring at the ceiling. What fuels this persistent worry? Often, it's the feeling of uncertainty or a sense of not being in control of your financial destiny. It's like walking through a maze blindfolded, where every turn feels uncertain and fraught with potential pitfalls.

The roots of financial anxiety can often be traced back to early experiences with money. Maybe you saw your parents arguing about bills, or perhaps you experienced financial hardship firsthand. As you take on more financial responsibilities, these moments can plant seeds of worry that grow into gnarly vines of anxiety. The good news? Just as these patterns are learned, they can also be unlearned or managed with the right strategies.

Developing Coping Mechanisms: Tools to Tame the Beast

When financial worries start knocking, don't let them set up camp. One of the first tools in your stress-busting toolkit should be mindfulness. It's not just for yogis or meditation enthusiasts; it's a practical tool for anyone. Mindfulness involves staying present and engaged in the moment rather than letting your mind catastrophize about future financial woes. Try this: the next time you catch yourself spiraling into worry, pause. Breathe deeply, focus on the sensations around you, and gently guide your thoughts back to the present. This practice can help break the cycle of anxiety, providing a mental reset button that keeps financial stress from overwhelming you.

Another powerful tool is proactive financial planning. This doesn't mean you need a spreadsheet for every dollar (unless that's your jam). Rather, you need to establish a clear plan for your income and expenses. Use budgeting apps or spreadsheets or simply write it down on paper—whatever works to give you a clear picture of where your money is going. This clarity can be incredibly soothing to a worried mind, as it replaces uncertainty with structure and predictability.

Setting Realistic Financial Goals: Your Anxiety-Reducing Compass

Setting wildly ambitious financial goals can be as stressful as an over-packed weekend itinerary. There's a place for ambition, but your everyday financial goals should be more like a leisurely stroll than a sprint. Start small. Maybe your first goal is to track your spending for a month or save a small emergency fund of $500. Achieving these smaller goals can provide a sense of accomplishment and build your confidence, making larger goals feel more attainable.

Tailoring your goals to your current life phase and capacity is also crucial. If you're a student or early in your career, your focus might be on slowly building savings or managing student loans rather than investing heavily or buying property. Aligning your goals with your real-life circumstances can prevent feelings of frustration and inade-quacy, which are often at the heart of financial anxiety.

Seeking Professional Help: When to Call in the Reinforcements

Just as you'd consult a doctor for a persistent cough, sometimes you need a professional to manage financial stress. How do you know when it's time to seek help? Here's a rule of thumb: if financial worries are keeping you up at night, affecting your relationships, or leading to physical symptoms like headaches or stomach issues, it might be time to talk to a professional. This could be a financial advisor who can help you create a more effective financial plan or a therapist who specializes in financial stress. Remember that seeking help is not a sign of weakness but a proactive step toward regaining your financial peace of mind.

Financial health, much like physical or emotional health, requires attention and care. By understanding the roots of financial anxiety, employing practical coping mechanisms, setting realistic goals, and knowing when to seek professional help, you can protect your financial future and keep your mental health in check. Just like that roller coaster, with the right strategies, you can ensure that your financial life has more ups than downs and that you enjoy the ride a whole lot more.

9.2 STAYING SAFE IN THE DIGITAL FINANCE WORLD

Imagine that you're navigating a bustling digital cityscape—neon signs flashing credit card deals, pop-up ads offering the latest investment tips, and sleek apps that promise the world with just a swipe. Welcome to the digital finance frontier, a place where managing your money is conveniently at your fingertips, but so are the myriad risks that lurk in the electronic shadows. Here, protecting your financial information isn't just about setting a strong password (although that's a start); it's about equipping yourself with a full arsenal of tools and knowledge to safeguard your digital dollars.

Protecting Your Financial Information Online: Fortifying Your Digital Finances

In today's digital age, safeguarding your financial information is crucial. Here's how you can fortify your digital finances:

1. Secure Your Transactions

- Use secure networks for online purchases and accessing financial accounts
- Avoid public Wi-Fi for sensitive transactions
- Verify website legitimacy before entering payment information
- Look for "https" in URLs (the 's' stands for secure)
- Be cautious of poorly designed websites or those with typos

It's like checking the safety gear before a skydive; you want to make sure everything is legit before you jump.

If the worst happens, and you find yourself scammed, it's not game over. First, take a deep breath—it happens to the best of us. Then, spring into action. Contact your bank or credit card company to report the fraud. They can block your card to prevent further unauthorized transactions and may help recover any lost funds. Next, change your online passwords, especially if you suspect they might have been compromised. Report the scam to organizations like the Federal Trade Commission in the U.S. or other relevant authorities in your country. They can't always get your money back, but they can take action to prevent others from falling victim.

Staying informed is your best defense. Scams evolve constantly, and keeping up-to-date on the latest schemes can help you stay one step ahead. Follow reputable tech blogs, subscribe to cybersecurity newsletters, and participate in community forums. Knowledge is power, and in the digital world, it's also your best protector.

Navigating the digital world's dangers doesn't need to be an impossible mission. Equipped with the right knowledge and tools, you can protect yourself from the majority of online threats. Keep your wits about you, trust your instincts, and remember that if something sounds too good to be true, it probably is.

Cryptocurrency Safety: Securing Your Digital Gold

Cryptocurrencies, the digital gold of the internet era, speak to the tech-savvy treasure hunter in all of us. Whether you're dabbling in Bitcoin, Ethereum, or any other crypto, remember that with great digital power comes great responsibility. Cryptocurrencies are stored in digital wallets, and these wallets can be as vulnerable as your physical wallet if not properly secured. Use digital wallets that allow you to keep control of your keys—a set of cryptographic information that lets you access your currency. Think of these keys as the combination to a safe. Store them somewhere secure, not just on a sticky note by your computer.

Moreover, when trading or mining crypto, use reputable exchanges, and keep an eye out for security features like cold storage options, which store the cryptocurrency offline and safe from potential online breaches. Remember that the value of cryptocurrencies can be as volatile as a ride on the stock market—exciting, sure, but with potential drops that aren't for the faint of heart.

9.3 FINANCIALLY PREPARING FOR LIFE'S UNEXPECTED EVENTS

Let's face it—life loves to throw curveballs. One day, you're sailing smoothly, and the next, you're hit with a job loss or a medical emergency that feels more like a strikeout. It's like playing a game of dodgeball blindfolded—you never know when a ball might come flying in your direction. That's why having a game plan for those "just in case" moments isn't only smart; it's essential for keeping your sanity and your savings intact.

The Importance of Emergency Planning: Why It's Your Financial BFF

Imagine this: you're heading home after your last final of the semester, and then, out of nowhere, your car decides to break down in the middle of nowhere. Panic mode, right? Now, if you had roadside assistance or a spare tire ready, that hiccup wouldn't turn into a holiday horror story. That's what an emergency fund does for your financial life. It prepares you for those unexpected breakdowns along the way, ensuring that they're just pit stops, not the end of the road.

Building an emergency fund isn't about being pessimistic; it's about being realistic. Life is unpredictable, and job security can sometimes feel as stable as a house of cards. A robust emergency fund acts like a financial shock absorber, helping you navigate through life's ups and downs without derailing your long-term financial goals. It's the buffer that keeps you from racking up debt when life decides to spice things up.

Insurance as a Safety Net: Not All Heroes Wear Capes

While your emergency fund is there to catch you when you fall, insurance is there to make sure you don't fall too hard. Health insurance is like your health guardian, stepping in when medical bills threaten. Then there's disability insurance, the protector of your income, ensuring that an accident or illness doesn't derail your financial stability. Let's not forget life insurance, the silent guardian for those you might leave behind, providing financial support in your absence.

Each type of insurance serves a unique role in your financial safety net. Without them, you're essentially walking a tightrope with no safety harness. Not an ideal scenario, right? By transferring significant financial risks to an insurance company, you reduce the burden on your emergency fund and ensure that a bump in the road doesn't turn into a full-blown financial crash.

Creating a Financial Contingency Plan: Your Blueprint for the Unexpected

Now, let's talk about stitching all these pieces together into a comprehensive financial contingency plan. This plan is your blueprint for handling financial emergencies—it outlines what steps to take, who to contact, and which resources to tap into when things go south.

Start by listing all your financial accounts, insurance policies, and emergency contacts. Note the passwords or answers to challenge questions, too. Choose a very safe place to keep all this private information.

Next, communicate your plan. If you have family or a partner, make sure they know where to find this information and understand what to do in case you're unable to manage your finances. It's like rehearsing an emergency drill—you hope you never need it, but you'll feel a heck of a lot better knowing it's there.

Regularly update this plan as your financial situation evolves. Got a new job? Update it. Paid off a loan? Update it. The more current your plan, the more effective it'll be when it's needed. Remember that the goal here isn't to obsess over what could go wrong; it's to feel empowered and ready for whatever comes your way.

By building a robust emergency fund, investing in the right insurance, and crafting a detailed financial contingency plan, you're not just preparing for the unexpected—you're ensuring that whatever life throws at you, you're ready to catch it, deal with it, and move on.

9.4 CONTINUOUS LEARNING IN PERSONAL FINANCE

Think of personal finance as your own blockbuster movie series, where every new release (or phase of your life) comes with different challenges and adventures. Just when you think you've mastered the basics—BOOM!—life throws in a twist, like a new tax regulation, an investment opportunity, or a revolutionary financial app. That's why treating financial education as a one-off event is like walking out of the theater mid-movie; you miss out on how the story evolves. The truth is that the landscape of personal finance is ever-changing, and staying informed is the only way to keep your finances in blockbuster shape.

Why is ongoing education in personal finance so important? It keeps you agile and prepared. Financial norms evolve, new financial products emerge, and economic conditions fluctuate. Each stage of your life will bring new financial decisions—buying a home, investing in stocks, saving for retirement. Continuous learning equips you with the knowledge to make informed decisions and to adapt strategies that fit your evolving needs. It's about staying relevant in the game of money, ensuring you're not making decisions based on outdated rules.

Now, let's talk about resources. The world is teeming with knowledge, and thanks to the internet, much of it is right at your fingertips. For those hungry to deepen their financial understanding, a myriad of books, podcasts, and websites offer great insights. Start with books that tackle broad financial principles or that delve into specific topics like investing or debt management.

Websites like *Investopedia*, *NerdWallet*, or *The Financial Diet* make learning about personal finance approachable and practical. They break down complex topics into digestible articles that cater to beginners and seasoned finance buffs alike. These platforms often update their content to reflect current trends and changes in the financial landscape, helping you stay on top of your financial game without feeling overwhelmed.

Why stop at digital resources? Attending workshops and seminars offers distinct benefits, too. These events provide a dynamic learning environment where you can interact with experts and peers. Whether it's an in-person retirement planning seminar or an online budgeting workshop, these sessions can offer personalized advice and answer specific questions you might have. Plus, they often provide networking opportunities that could lead to mentorships or professional relationships beneficial to your financial journey.

Part of learning is sharing—that's where the real mastery of knowledge comes in. Sharing what you've learned about personal finance with your community not only cements your own understanding but also uplifts those around you. Whether it's explaining the basics of budgeting to a friend or starting a blog about your investment journey, teaching others allows you to refine your knowledge and spot gaps in your understanding. It's a win-win: you reinforce your learning and help others navigate their financial landscapes more confidently.

As we wrap up this chapter, consider continuous learning in personal finance not just as a tool for personal empowerment, but also as a key for fostering a financially literate society. The more you learn and share, the better equipped you become to make sound financial decisions, adapting to the ever-changing economic environment with ease and confidence.

ACTION STEPS FOR PROTECTING YOUR FINANCIAL FUTURE

1. Nurturing Your Financial Mental Health

- Identify Financial Anxiety: Recognize and understand the root causes of your financial worries.
- Practice Mindfulness: Use mindfulness techniques to stay present and manage financial stress.
- Create a Budget: Establish a clear budget to understand and control your income and expenses.
- Set Realistic Goals: Define achievable financial goals that match your current life stage.
- Seek Professional Help: Consult a financial advisor or therapist if financial anxiety significantly impacts your well-being.

2. Staying Safe in the Digital Finance World

- Use Strong Passwords: Ensure that all your financial accounts are protected with strong, unique passwords.
- Enable Two-Factor Authentication: Add an extra layer of security to your accounts.

- Regularly Update Software: Keep your financial apps and software up-to-date to protect against vulnerabilities.
- Be Wary of Phishing: Avoid clicking on suspicious links or sharing personal information online.
- Stay Informed: Keep up with the latest cybersecurity practices and digital finance scams.

3. Financially Preparing for Life's Unexpected Events

- Build an Emergency Fund: Save 3-6 months' worth of living expenses in an accessible account.
- Get Insurance: Ensure that you have adequate health, disability, and life insurance to cover potential risks.
- Create a Contingency Plan: Document your financial accounts, insurance policies, and emergency contacts.
- Communicate Your Plan: Make sure your family understands and can access your contingency plan.
- Review and Update Regularly: Periodically update your contingency plan to reflect any changes in your financial situation.

4. Continuous Learning in Personal Finance

- Read Financial Books: Stay informed by reading books on personal finance and investing.
- Listen to Podcasts: Subscribe to finance-related podcasts to gain insights during your commute or free time.
- Use Online Resources: Regularly visit reputable financial websites for up-to-date information.
- Attend Workshops and Seminars: Participate in events to learn from experts and to network with peers.
- Share Knowledge: Teach others about personal finance to reinforce your understanding and to help your community.

KEEPING THE GAME ALIVE

Now that you have everything you need to master money management, avoid costly mistakes, invest like a pro, and secure your financial future, it's time to pass on your newfound knowledge and show other readers where they can find the same help.

Simply by leaving your honest opinion of this book on Amazon, you'll show other teens and young adults where they can find the information they're looking for. Your review could change their lives forever!

Thank you for your help. Financial literacy is kept alive when we pass on our knowledge – and you're helping us to do just that.

Scan the QR code to leave your review on Amazon

https://amzn.to/472gr69

CONCLUSION: YOUR JOURNEY TO FINANCIAL EMPOWERMENT

As you reach the end of this guide, remember that financial literacy is not a destination, but a continuous journey. You've taken the first significant steps by diving into the essentials of money management, from budgeting and saving to investing and understanding taxes. Each chapter has equipped you with the tools and knowledge needed to navigate the often complex world of finance with confidence and clarity.

Reflect on where you started—perhaps feeling overwhelmed by financial jargon or unsure about making the right money decisions. Now, envision your future self: confident, informed, and ready to take charge of your financial destiny. Whether it's setting up a robust budget, opening your first investment account, or simply understanding your paycheck, every skill you've learned here contributes to building a secure and prosperous future.

Remember that the goal is not just to avoid financial pitfalls but also to thrive financially. Stay curious, keep learning, and adapt as you go. The financial landscape will continue to evolve, but with the foundation you've built through this book, you'll be prepared to handle whatever comes your way. Embrace the journey, continue to seek knowledge, and most importantly, apply what you've learned.

Financial freedom is within your reach. With dedication and the right mindset, you can achieve the financial independence you dream of. Go ahead, take control, and make your financial future as bright and secure as possible. Your journey has just begun, and the possibilities are endless.

REFERENCES

Financial Literacy for Teens: How to Teach Your Teen. (n.d.). Washington Federal. Retrieved from https://www.wafdbank.com/blog/family-finance/financial-literacy-for-teens

How to Budget With a Low Income. (n.d.). Ramsey Solutions. Retrieved from https://www.ramseysolutions.com/budgeting/how-to-budget-money-with-low-income

Introduction to Investing. (n.d.). Investor.gov. Retrieved from https://www.investor.gov/introduction-investing

7 Common Banking Fees and How to Avoid Them. (n.d.). Experian. Retrieved from https://www.experian.com/blogs/ask-experian/how-to-avoid-bank-fees/

The Best Money Apps for Kids and Teens in 2024. (n.d.). Dough Roller. Retrieved from https://www.doughroller.net/best-money-apps-for-kids-and-teens

8 Financial Tips for Young Adults. (n.d.). Investopedia. Retrieved from https://www.investopedia.com/articles/younginvestors/08/eight-tips.asp

How To Save Money In College: 50 Different Ideas To Try. (n.d.). The College Investor. Retrieved from https://thecollegeinvestor.com/22453/save-money-in-college/

Omololu, E. (2024, March 15). 9 Financial Mistakes To Avoid In Your 20s And 30s. Forbes. Retrieved from https://www.forbes.com/sites/enochomololu/2024/03/15/9-financial-mistakes-to-avoid-in-your-20s-and-30s/

Emergency Fund Calculator – Forbes Advisor. (n.d.). Forbes. Retrieved from https://www.forbes.com/advisor/banking/emergency-fund-calculator/#:~:

High-yield savings account vs. traditional savings account: Which is better? (n.d.). Yahoo Finance. Retrieved from https://finance.yahoo.com/personal-finance/high-yield-savings-account-vs-traditional-savings-account-which-is-better-120024972.html

Washington Federal. (n.d.). Financial literacy for teens: How to teach your teen. Retrieved from https://www.wafdbank.com/blog/family-finance/financial-literacy-for-teens

Ramsey Solutions. (n.d.). How to budget with a low income. Retrieved from https://www.ramseysolutions.com/budgeting/how-to-budget-money-with-low-income

Investor.gov. (n.d.). Introduction to investing. Retrieved from https://www.investor.gov/introduction-investing

Experian. (n.d.). 7 common banking fees and how to avoid them. Retrieved from https://www.experian.com/blogs/ask-experian/how-to-avoid-bank-fees/

Dough Roller. (n.d.). The best money apps for kids and teens in 2024. Retrieved from https://www.doughroller.net/best-money-apps-for-kids-and-teens

Investopedia. (n.d.). 8 financial tips for young adults. Retrieved from https://www.investopedia.com/articles/younginvestors/08/eight-tips.asp

The College Investor. (n.d.). How to save money in college: 50 different ideas to try. Retrieved from https://thecollegeinvestor.com/22453/save-money-in-college/

Omololu, E. (2024, March 15). 9 financial mistakes to avoid in your 20s and 30s. Forbes. Retrieved from https://www.forbes.com/sites/enochomololu/2024/03/15/9-financial-mistakes-to-avoid-in-your-20s-and-30s/

Forbes. (n.d.). Emergency fund calculator – Forbes advisor. Retrieved from https://www.forbes.com/advisor/banking/emergency-fund-calculator/#:

Yahoo Finance. (n.d.). High-yield savings account vs. traditional savings account: Which is better? Retrieved from https://finance.yahoo.com/personal-finance/high-yield-savings-account-vs-traditional-savings-account-which-is-better-120024972.html

FlexJobs. (n.d.). The gig economy: Definition, pros & cons, and finding jobs. Retrieved from https://www.flexjobs.com/blog/post/what-is-the-gig-economy-v2/

Upwork. (n.d.). How to become a freelancer in 2024: The complete guide. Retrieved from https://www.upwork.com/resources/how-to-become-a-freelancer

Investopedia. (n.d.). 10 successful young entrepreneurs. Retrieved from https://www.investopedia.com/10-successful-young-entrepreneurs-4773310

Internal Revenue Service. (n.d.). How to file your taxes: Step by step. Retrieved from https://www.irs.gov/how-to-file-your-taxes-step-by-step

Internal Revenue Service. (n.d.). Credits and deductions for individuals. Retrieved from https://www.irs.gov/credits-and-deductions-for-individuals

Internal Revenue Service. (n.d.). Gig economy tax center. Retrieved from https://www.irs.gov/businesses/gig-economy-tax-center

TurboTax. (n.d.). Taxes for grads: Do scholarships count as taxable income? Retrieved from https://turbotax.intuit.com/tax-tips/college-and-education/taxes-for-grads-do-scholarships-count-as-taxable-income/L2hWn0lpe#:~

Discover. (n.d.). How to create a financial vision board. Retrieved from https://www.discover.com/online-banking/banking-topics/financial-vision-board/

Investopedia. (n.d.). Insurance: Definition, how it works, and main types of insurance. Retrieved from https://www.investopedia.com/terms/i/insurance.asp

Edward Jones. (n.d.). How to save money for big purchases. Retrieved from https://www.edwardjones.com/us-en/market-news-insights/investor-education/investment-age/big-purchases

TheStreet. (n.d.). Why you need a financial roadmap and how to build one. Retrieved from https://www.thestreet.com/retirement-daily/your-money/why-you-need-a-financial-roadmap-and-how-to-build-one

Wise. (n.d.). The 9 best online banks in 2023. Retrieved from https://wise.com/us/blog/best-online-bank

NerdWallet. (n.d.). Best investing apps of May 2024. Retrieved from https://www.nerdwallet.com/best/investing/investment-apps

CNBC Select. (n.d.). 5 tips on what to look for when choosing a budgeting app. Retrieved from https://www.cnbc.com/select/what-to-look-for-in-budgeting-app/

Federal Deposit Insurance Corporation. (2021, October). Avoiding scams and scammers. Retrieved from https://www.fdic.gov/resources/consumers/consumer-news/2021-10.html

HelpGuide. (n.d.). Coping with financial stress. Retrieved from https://www.helpguide.org/articles/stress/coping-with-financial-stress.htm

U.S. Bank. (n.d.). Mindset matters: How to practice mindful spending. Retrieved from https://www.usbank.com/financialiq/manage-your-household/personal-finance/how-to-practice-mindful-spending.html

Investors Cabin. (n.d.). The impact of social media on teen spending habits. Retrieved from https://investorscabin.com/articles/the-impact-of-social-media-on-teen-spending-habits

Consumer Financial Protection Bureau. (n.d.). An essential guide to building an emergency fund. Retrieved from https://www.consumerfinance.gov/an-essential-guide-to-building-an-emergency-fund/

Annuity.org. (n.d.). Financial literacy statistics. Retrieved from https://www.annuity.org/financial-literacy/financial-literacy-statistics

Berger, R. (n.d.). Round up apps. Retrieved from https://robberger.com/round-up-apps

Consumer Financial Protection Bureau. (n.d.). An essential guide to building an emergency fund. Retrieved from https://www.consumerfinance.gov/an-essential-guide-to-building-an-emergency-fund/

Protective. (n.d.). What freelancers need to know about taxes in the gig economy. Retrieved from https://www.protective.com/learn/what-freelancers-need-to-know-about-taxes-in-the-gig-economy

LegalZoom. (n.d.). Commonly missed tax deductions for gig workers. Retrieved from https://www.legalzoom.com/articles/commonly-missed-tax-deductions-for-gig-workers

Investopedia. (n.d.). One thing gig workers need to know about tax liability. Retrieved from https://www.investopedia.com/fa-one-thing-gig-worker-tax-liability-8621932

TurboTax. (n.d.). Side giggers: Tax tips for side jobs. Retrieved from https://turbotax.intuit.com/tax-tips/self-employment-taxes/side-giggers-tax-tips-for-side-jobs/L6025l8Uh

Super Lawyers. (n.d.). How to do your taxes in the gig economy. Retrieved from https://www.superlawyers.com/resources/tax/new-york/how-to-do-your-taxes-in-the-gig-economy/

www.ingramcontent.com/pod-product-compliance
Lightning Source LLC
Chambersburg PA
CBHW071325210326
41597CB00015B/1355